# REAL ESTATE INVESTING

in Plain English

DEFINITIONS.
EXAMPLES.
USES.

# REAL ESTATE INVESTING

## in Plain English

**DEFINITIONS.
EXAMPLES.
USES.**

John A. Yoegel, PhD

Adams Media

New York  Amsterdam/Antwerp  London  Toronto  Sydney/Melbourne  New Delhi

# ▲adamsmedia

Adams Media
An Imprint of Simon & Schuster, LLC
100 Technology Center Drive
Stoughton, MA 02072

First Adams Media hardcover edition
December 2025

ADAMS MEDIA and colophon are registered trademarks of Simon & Schuster, LLC.

For information about special discounts for bulk purchases, please contact Simon & Schuster Special Sales at 1-866-506-1949 or business@simonandschuster.com.

The Simon & Schuster Speakers Bureau can bring authors to your live event. For more information or to book an event, contact the Simon & Schuster Speakers Bureau at 1-866-248-3049 or visit our website at www.simonspeakers.com.

Interior design by Maya Caspi
Images © Adobe Stock/Abbasy Kautsar, Icons-Studio

Manufactured in the United States of America

1 2025

Library of Congress Control Number: 2025943418

ISBN 978-1-5072-2513-4
ISBN 978-1-5072-2514-1 (ebook)

# Contents

# Introduction

Understanding all the pieces of real estate investing can be hard—and confusing. To succeed, you need to adopt the terms that successful real estate investors are using. For example, you need to know language relating to selecting the right property for you, how to purchase the property, and how to evaluate your financials throughout your investing journey. These terms (and many more) are the building blocks of your success in this form of investing, and so it helps to have them explained in a way that makes sense.

That's where *Real Estate Investing in Plain English* comes in. Here you'll find more than 300 glossary terms that define and clarify any real estate investing language you'll come across. After all, whether you're a seasoned pro or someone just starting to invest, sometimes an easy-to-understand explanation to guide or teach you is exactly what's needed—which is why each glossary term is so simple to follow. First, each term is quickly summarized. Then, the "What it is" section provides a clear definition. Next, the "How it works" section further contextualizes and explains the concept. Finally, the "How it is used" example uses the term in an everyday sentence.

Throughout the book, you'll find the glossary terms grouped into common real estate investing categories that will help you understand each term in context. For example:

- **Chapter 1: Types of Property** includes terms like *commercial property, manufactured home,* and *raw land.*
- **Chapter 3: Financing** provides definitions for *ARM (adjustable rate mortgage), DTI (debt-to-income) ratio,* and *origination fee.*
- **Chapter 5: Leases** has lingo like *gross lease, market rent,* and *rent escalation clause.*
- **Chapter 8: Buying and Selling** includes *broker commission, negotiation,* and *title search.*
- **Chapter 11: Governmental Issues** gives you terms such as *affordable housing mandate, green building,* and *zoning laws.*
- And there are plenty more!

Ultimately, whether you need a refresher on real estate tax terminology or want to know what terms to use when you're dealing with maintenance on your property, *Real Estate Investing in Plain English* will help you understand the complexities of this type of investing and more. Using this book, you can take confident steps to build wealth, successfully navigate the investment arena, and effectively protect the economic future you're working so hard to create. The clear information in this book will help you manage your real estate investing goals easily and successfully.

# CHAPTER 1

# Types of Property

Investing in real estate can be an effective and prosperous financial decision, but it takes skill and knowledge to determine which properties to invest in. Using this book, you'll learn some of the different ways you can profit from buying a property. However, before you learn about these more advanced strategies, this chapter begins with the various types of property that you might invest in.

It's important to note that some properties require specialized knowledge, while others need significant management. Still, other types may offer income with very little effort.

Essentially, any property that can be purchased and that will generate a profit either short-term or long-term is an investment property. This chapter will present information about properties that are familiar to you (like multifamily homes), as well as some you may never have thought of as investments, like mobile homes. Let's begin the investigation of the many types of investment properties there are to offer!

## agricultural property

land used for farming and grazing

**What it is:** properties in this category are used to produce what might be called natural products, or products directly related to the land, rather than manufactured products (like from a factory)

**How it works:** Agricultural properties support growing food crops such as wheat or corn. They are also used for raising animals such as cows and sheep. Additionally, these properties may grow plants like flowers and Christmas trees. In theory, you could buy agricultural property and become a farmer, but a real estate investor would buy this property and rent it to a farmer or cattle rancher. The person renting the land could be someone new to the area or the farmer next door who is looking to increase their operation.

**How it is used:** Haru may not know anything about farming, but he knows that good **agricultural property** around here rents for top dollar.

## amenities

extra facilities a property owner might provide to their tenants

**What it is:** a landlord (the property owner) might enhance their building with extra incentives in order to attract tenants

**How it works:** A building owner, the landlord, wants to keep their building full and attract tenants quickly when there is vacant space. So, some landlords offer the tenants something extra in the building that these renters and/or building employees can use. In office buildings, landlords may include gyms, quiet rooms, and food courts. Residential landlords might offer a swimming pool, meeting rooms, and outdoor garden spaces. An amenity is something above and beyond the minimum tenant expectations but may become more common as landlords compete for tenants.

**How it is used:** Since the rent was the same, the office manager compared the **amenities** offered by the two landlords in deciding where to move the new offices.

## apartment

**a place someone pays rent to live in**

**What it is:** a rentable private living space located within a building, which may be divided into two or more of these individual spaces (units)

**How it works:** Apartments are individual spaces within buildings specifically designed for people to live in. The person (or people) renting the apartment, the tenant(s), will have exclusive use of that space without having to share anything like kitchens or bathrooms with the outside population. Depending on the design of the building, the tenant may have their own private entrance or have to go through a lobby or hallway. Even though the term *apartment* describes a physical space, it also commonly means someone pays rent to use it and does not own it, unlike a condominium or cooperative apartment (co-op). Buildings having four to six or more apartments are usually called apartment buildings or apartment houses.

**How it is used:** The couple decided to rent an **apartment** for a year while saving to buy a house.

## apartment complex

**several buildings with residential rental units under one ownership**

**What it is:** a group of 2+ buildings, each with 2+ rental units, owned by one person or corporation

**How it works:** Investors sometimes purchase and operate apartment complexes—a single piece of property that contains more than one apartment building—as a matter of efficiency. Rather than owning several buildings in different locations, investors can then focus their rental operation in one place. This can create efficiencies in management and operations such as staffing, maintenance, and response to tenant complaints. These complexes may also allow for more green space, playgrounds, and other tenant amenities that are shared between the buildings. The individual buildings in an apartment complex may be much larger or smaller in size than others.

**How it is used:** The XYZ Corporation decided to buy the three-building **apartment complex** rather than single buildings in three different locations.

## commercial property

### land or building used for business purposes

**What it is:** properties divided into different use categories (like business or commerce) by government regulations (rules/procedures from the government) and by actual use

**How it works:** Whether owned or rented, people must have a place to conduct business. Whether it's selling groceries or seeing patients, places exist where people can come together to provide and receive services or goods. These commercial properties have different needs than places where people live (residential properties). They may need extensive parking, to be in areas convenient to highways or public transportation, and likely to be away from residential areas. The buildings are designed to accommodate their use; for example, a doctor's office is not going to be designed like a restaurant or a grocery store.

**How it is used:** The investor owned quite a few residential properties and decided that they were ready to buy their first **commercial property**.

## condominium

### owning space in a building without directly owning the land

**What it is:** a legal form of property ownership where a person individually owns the space within a building but not the building or land itself

**How it works:** In a condominium (also informally called a condo), the owner has full ownership of their space but limited ownership rights to the building itself, which is usually owned in common with others who own similar individual spaces. It could be a residential building where the owner owns an apartment, or in a commercial building where the person may own an office. The building itself as well as the land under and surrounding it is owned in common by all the condominium owners.

There is a monthly fee for maintenance of the building and grounds. This fee is usually referred to as a homeowners association (HOA) fee in residential condominiums and common area maintenance (CAM) charges in commercial condominiums.

**How it is used:** The couple decided to purchase a **condominium** instead of renting an apartment for their first home.

## cooperative

### a form of real estate ownership

**What it is:** a different way to own real estate than conventional ownership; like condominium ownership, there are a group of other owners involved

**How it works:** Cooperative (otherwise called co-op) ownership is where a corporation owns a building and sells shares in the corporation. The shares allow a person to occupy a unit in the building using a proprietary lease. A proprietary lease is unique in that it's tied to ownership of shares in a corporation rather than a standard lease, which has no ownership rights. Technically, the shares in the corporation are personal property rather than real estate. Cooperatives may be either residential or commercial, and they can be financed in a way similar to a conventional mortgage loan.

**How it is used:** The board of directors of the **cooperative** approved the new tenants.

## franchise location

### a property rented to a franchise business

**What it is:** franchise businesses, whether restaurants or other types of businesses, require locations in which to operate; this investment type involves buying property and renting it to the franchisee (owner/operator of the franchise)

**How it works:** Franchisees can either own or lease the property on which to build their franchise building. As an investment, a property owner can lease the property to the franchise owner with a land lease. These properties may have certain requirements necessary to the franchise, such as the ability to construct a drive-through lane at a fast-food franchise. The property owner may have nothing to do with the operation of the franchise business.

**How it is used:** They had secured the franchise rights and now had to find an approved **franchise location** to build their restaurant.

## historic building

### a property that has significance due to its past

**What it is:** a building that has been designated by the government to be preserved for its significance to some person or event in history

**How it works:** Designated historic buildings will usually have government regulations imposed on them. These regulations typically involve exterior restoration work. Typically, the restoration work must be done using materials and designs that preserve the original architectural character of the building. Restoration can be expensive due to the specialized materials and workmanship that may be required. Interior restoration is not often regulated but can be under certain circumstances. Entire neighborhoods, as well as individual properties, may be designated as historic.

**How it is used:** The investor wanted to buy the **historic building** but was concerned about the cost and special permissions needed for restoration.

## industrial property

### places for manufacturing and storage uses

**What it is:** a site designed to accommodate use for "industry," meaning the manufacture, storage, and/or shipping of anything from cars to computer chips

**How it works:** Industrial properties usually require special conditions. They are located away from residential areas, have access to major highways, and are large enough to buffer noise and odors from whatever is happening on the property. There may be a single building site or a grouping of different uses on a single property. These are sometimes called industrial parks. These parks may be under single ownership with individual properties leased to various tenants. Alternately, individual sites may be separately owned but managed as a single property by an investor who retains an ownership interest of interior roads, buffer areas, and one or more individual sites. These parks contain individual properties that may not be compatible with other parts of a community. For example, a radio station may need a radio tower (not useful to anyone else). Industrial uses may include warehouses, storage, and shipping facilities.

**How it is used:** ABC Construction Company was interested in finding an **industrial property** in which it could store its equipment.

## land

### the surface of the earth with or without structures

**What it is:** the portion of the world without a body of water; it may or may not be utilized

**How it works:** The idea behind owning land entails something called the bundle of rights. It's a very simple concept that says within certain legal limits you can do anything, nothing, or many things with the land at the same time. So, you can give someone the right to build a building on your land, someone else the right to drill for oil, and a third person the right to cross your land to get to their property. And you can get paid for each of those things while retaining ownership of your land.

There are many categorizations of land. Land without anything on it is called "vacant land." If it has a building on it, real estate investors call it "improved" or "developed" land. "Raw land" refers to natural or undeveloped land, and a "site" is an area where a building is planned.

**How it is used:** They bought the building and the piece of **land** next to it so they could expand their business.

## land investment

### buying undeveloped land as a way to generate income

**What it is:** an investor will buy land with the intention of profiting from it

**How it works:** Land allows for several possibilities for profit. One is the buy-and-hold strategy of allowing supply and demand to gradually drive up value. Another is to take some legal action such as a rezoning (changing to a more valuable zone) or subdivision (dividing into multiple lots) that will likely increase the value of the land. Finally, the investor can develop the property according to local needs and government regulations. The property can then be sold or operated for rental income.

**How it is used:** As the community grew, the investors saw the possibility of profiting by making a **land investment** with a parcel of land located at the edge of town.

## manufactured home

a house built somewhere other than its final location

**What it is:** entire houses or large parts of houses can be constructed off-site from their final location; the final assembly takes place at the location (called a lot or site)

**How it works:** Modular homes are a type of manufactured housing, as they are constructed off-site. Boxes are built in a factory, shipped to the building lot, and assembled there. Panelized houses will have large sections of walls constructed off-site, shipped to the site, and placed onto the final home. Another type of manufactured home is the precut, which has the conventional pieces of a house cut to size before delivery for construction at the house site. In all cases, construction and materials must meet local building code requirements.

**How it is used:** Before choosing a **manufactured home** company, it's a good idea to visit the factory where the home's components are made to ensure the quality meets expectations.

## mixed-use property

a space or building containing different uses

**What it is:** a site that can, subject to government regulations (rules/procedures from the government), be developed with several different uses in mind

**How it works:** Properties, especially in urban areas, usually have several stories (floors). While most zoning tends to allow only one use per property, vibrant downtown areas benefit from one building having many uses. For example, a mixed-use building (sometimes called multi-use) might have retail stores on the first floor, several levels of offices above that, and residential units above the offices. Two-story buildings in smaller communities might have a store on the first floor and an apartment or office on the second floor. As an investment, mixed-use properties allow the investor to be involved in two markets, like retail and residential, in one property. In some parts of the country, these smaller, multi-use buildings are called "taxpayers."

**How it is used:** The clothing store owner bought a **mixed-use property** to locate their store as well as generate income from the offices on the second floor.

## mobile home

### a dwelling unit that can be moved from place to place

**What it is:** a type of manufactured home that is built on a vehicle frame and can be towed into place on a piece of property

**How it works:** Mobile homes are buildings constructed with wheels, meant to move, and they are fully built at a factory. There is no on-site construction needed except to connect to utilities such as water, sewer, and power. Although they can be towed on their own wheels, the usual arrangement is to place them on a foundation on a privately owned lot or in a mobile home park where multiple units are located. In a mobile home park, the mobile home itself can be rented but is more usually bought and sold. The spot on which it is fixed is rented by the mobile home park owner to the tenant owner of the mobile home. The investment potential here is in owning the mobile home park.

**How it is used:** We decided to buy a **mobile home** for the time being until we can save enough for a regular house.

## multifamily home

### a building that has more than one dwelling unit in it

**What it is:** residential buildings are classified both legally and in common usage as single-family and multifamily dwellings

**How it works:** Any building containing two or more dwelling units would be considered a multifamily home for legal purposes. Buildings having two, three, and four units may have different names in various places. Duplex, triplex, quadplex, or fourplex are common designations in some areas. In these smaller multifamily homes, the owner often lives in one apartment while renting out the other units.

**How it is used:** The town took steps to designate areas near downtown for **multifamily homes**.

## office building

**a commercial building used to house offices**

**What it is:** a single building or group of buildings designed to provide private spaces to a variety of tenants whose work is primarily indoors, such as accountants and attorneys

**How it works:** Many businesses require private space to conduct their operations. They may wish to be in a downtown area or near some other building, such as attorneys wishing to be near a courthouse. They may require small or large space but seldom need enough space to own a building. So, renting space in a building housing multiple offices is the practical solution. These buildings often provide amenities such as cafeterias and gyms.

**How it is used:** The location of the **office building** near the train station made it easy for the workers who didn't have cars.

## office park

**a single location, outside of downtown, that has one or more office buildings**

**What it is:** a place under single ownership that provides office space to one or more tenants in a campus-like setting; the buildings are often low-rise (1–3 stories) and the property may resemble a college campus

**How it works:** Office buildings were once (and now again) primarily located downtown in what are often called "urban centers." As downtown areas became congested and dated, offices began to be built on vacant land outside of these downtown areas. An office park might be a single building headquarters of a company or multiple office buildings renting space to multiple tenants. There is plenty of parking, easy access off a highway, and green space around the building, creating a park-like setting. These sites are sometimes called office campuses.

**How it is used:** Since the company moved to the **office park**, I've been able to take a walk in the woods almost every day at lunch.

## property

### something that can be owned

**What it is:** the commonly used term to describe vacant land or land with a structure on it; it can also mean anything that can be owned and sold or exchanged

**How it works:** When talking about real estate, the precise term for property is *real property*, but it is seldom used. The word *property* is usually enough to describe a piece of real estate. To use the term differently, you might say "personal property," meaning something portable like a toaster or a car. Real property and personal property, like the house and the furniture within it, can both be part of a real estate deal.

**How it is used:** The broker showed the buyer a **property** that they thought would suit their needs.

## raw land

### land with no improvements on or near it

**What it is:** land that will need work in preparation to become a building site

**How it works:** Imagine a very large farm. To the farmer, this land is developed for its intended purpose. However, to a real estate developer, most of that farm is raw land with a few structures built on it. It has no internal road system. The nearest water lines (minus irrigation lines), sewer lines, and electricity may be miles away. The only upside is that it's probably flat. However, if this land was a forest, you would also have trees to contend with. This forest land is even *more* of an example of raw land, requiring extensive work before it will be suitable for building something like single-family homes.

**How it is used:** The developer decided to buy the farm because they saw the potential for turning **raw land** into a housing development.

## residential property

### property that is used or designated for use as a place where people live

**What it is:** one of the designations that governments provide to determine how a property can be utilized

**How it works:** Residential properties fall into different categories primarily by density, or how many dwelling units (apartments or houses) can be built on a given size piece of property. A very low-density area might allow one house on every four acres. A high-density area, say near downtown of a heavily populated city, might allow 200 units or more per acre. The term *residential* designates the actual use of the property (for example, homes). In the world of investing, terminology is often very local. In some areas, a building containing many dwelling units might be called a commercial property, primarily because it is bought, operated, and sold for investment purposes.

**How it is used:** The investor wanted to build homes, so they asked the broker to show them **residential properties.**

## single-family home

### a residence that is designed for one family

**What it is:** a house designed to allow one family to live comfortably with the usual amenities (or benefits)

**How it works:** A single-family home's definition does not say what a "typical family" looks like. Legal definitions according to government regulations (rules made by the governing power) determine the meaning of the term *family*. Since there are definitions for specific types of housing (like condominiums, apartments, and cooperatives), a single-family home has come to mean "a freestanding, single dwelling unit." In some markets, this term is also used to describe homes attached on one or both sides. *Unit* is a generic term that can be applied to any residential dwelling.

**How it is used:** The buyers had decided that it was time to sell their condominium and move into a **single-family home.**

## site

### property ready to be built on

**What it is:** land needs to be prepared before it can be built on, and any such preparations transform that land into a site

**How it works:** A site (or building site) is land transformed from its natural state to be built upon. Generally, a site will have legally acceptable access to it, like by road or easement approved by the local government. A site will have utilities like electricity, water, and sewer available to the property. Putting in roads and utilities is the major step needed to turn raw land into sites for building.

**How it is used:** They were lucky to have located the last building **site** in the development for their new home.

## townhouse

### type of single-family residence

**What it is:** a two-story, single-family residence attached to other houses on both sides

**How it works:** The term *townhouse* is an architectural description referring to houses designed in imitation of houses built in certain urban areas during the 1800s. Since some early condominium projects were built in the townhouse style, the words *townhouse* and *condominium* became interchangeable. In some markets, the term *townhouse* was used to describe any type of residential development where the residents owned their units, regardless of their architectural style.

**How it is used:** They considered buying a **townhouse** in the city.

## vacation home

### a home built in an area oriented toward getaways and tourists

**What it is:** this type of house may be a single-family or apartment-type unit generally used for only a portion of the year

**How it works:** Vacation homes as an investment may work in several ways. A developer might build homes in an area with attractions for people, such as beaches or skiing. These homes can be sold and used at will by the owners, even if only seasonally. A different developer might build such homes and rent them on a short- or long-term basis. An owner interested in this option would most likely hire professional management to run a hospitality (i.e., a hotel-type) business. The units could also be sold on a time-share (designated period of time) basis.

**How it is used:** The buyer is looking for a **vacation home** but wants it within a two-hour drive of where they live.

# CHAPTER 2

# Property Selection

Property selection is the key to making a successful real estate investment. No one can predict the future, which is why all investments carry some risk. What you can do, however, is minimize your risk by carefully selecting an investment property based on what you currently know, as well as what you can reasonably guess about the future. Knowing the language is an important first step.

This chapter presents terms and definitions that apply to many of the analytical aspects of selecting a property. Whether you are inexperienced as an investor or are considering a particular type of property that is new to you, you may want to consult an expert in various aspects of these property analyses. Even experienced investors will consult specialists like appraisers and engineers when considering a property for purchase.

These terms will help you understand some of the fine points to be considered when deciding on a real estate investment. They will also help you know what you need and what to ask for when consulting specialists about an investment property.

## asset class

### the type of investment

**What it is:** the type of investment (stocks, bonds, or real estate), and within real estate investing, it applies to the property type (residential or commercial)

**How it works:** Different asset classes within real estate investment carry different levels of risk, profitability, and management difficulty. For example, commercial property is generally considered to be more profitable than residential property. It also carries more risk as it is affected by various market conditions. Asset classes in the larger sense of an investment portfolio allow for considering various aspects of different investments and how they may affect the entire portfolio.

**How it is used:** Their real estate **asset classes** contain many properties.

## cap rate comparison

### a way to compare profitability among properties

**What it is:** when considering several investment properties, comparing the income that each will generate

**How it works:** The capitalization (cap) rate is the relationship between the cost of the property and the income it generates. All things being equal, the higher the cap rate, the more income a property will generate. If an investor can obtain the correct price and income data, they can calculate the cap rate. The property with the higher cap rate may not work as an investment for several reasons. For example, it may be too expensive for the investor.

**How it is used:** The **cap rate comparison** indicated the building with the 10% cap rate would be the best investment, but it needed a lot of work.

## code compliance

### the understanding that the property has obeyed (no violations of) all government codes

**What it is:** properties/buildings are subject to various government regulations (sometimes called codes); careful buyers/investors will review possible issues in complying with these codes

**How it works:** There are several government codes that apply to land development and buildings, ranging from zoning ordinances to drainage rules to building codes. Code compliance refers to an aspect of due diligence where the buyer examines all public records as well as the property itself to determine whether there are any existing or potential violations of these codes. Some violations may be easily dealt with; more serious ones may result in the buyer not buying the property. An investor looking at an apartment building may easily fix a fire code violation of insufficient fire extinguishers. However, code violations involving the presence of environmentally hazardous dumping on the property may be too costly for the buyer.

**How it is used:** The buyer found that the building was not in **code compliance** with the town safety code.

## diversification value

a way to spread investment risk

**What it is:** the concept of spreading, and therefore reducing, investment risk by investing in different types of assets

**How it works:** There are two levels of diversification value (minimizing risk in your investing portfolio) that can be considered. The first is diversification of your investments by investing in completely different classes of assets, like rental properties, stocks, bonds, and precious metals. The second type of diversification value is diversification of real estate investments. For example, you might own a residential rental property, an office building rental, and a small strip mall. You might also periodically engage in flipping a property. The idea is by spreading your risk, if market conditions go against one class of property (or investment type), they may not affect another class of property.

**How it is used:** The investor understood **diversification value** well enough to look for a mixed-use residential/commercial building for their first investment.

## due diligence

the research needed to make a good decision

**What it is:** the concept in any investment situation describing the reasonable amount of research needed to make a good decision

**How it works:** There are no hard-and-fast rules for performing due diligence in examining an investment. You should gather as much available information as possible to help make a good decision. For example, perhaps you wanted to buy a property with a pre-existing building. Due diligence would require you to examine records at the local building department to determine if there have been any additions or changes made to the structures on the property and if these changes were properly permitted and constructed. The buyer would also see if there were any building code violations that had been reported. Examining public records is an important part of due diligence since they are readily available.

**How it is used:** The buyer performed their **due diligence** with the help of their broker before deciding to buy the property.

## exit strategy

### how an investor ends their investments

**What it is:** an investor's clear need to decide what to do with their investment properties, including how to get out of them

**How it works:** When purchasing one or more investment properties, it's wise to plan an eventual exit strategy that gets the property out of your hands. The exit strategy for any property is subjected to the investor's goals, financial position, and personal issues. For example, an investor without heirs may want to sell all the properties before he dies, but an investor with heirs may leave the property in their estate. While owning a property, an investor may decide that when the property has a certain amount of equity, it will be sold to buy a larger property. Exit strategies should remain flexible based on changing real estate values, economic issues, and personal circumstances.

**How it is used:** The real estate investor put together an **exit strategy** for his investments so his family wouldn't have to deal with them.

## investment property

### a building primarily bought for income generation

**What it is:** virtually any site/building can be used to make money, and some don't have any other practical uses for the buyer

**How it works:** There are many properties that can be bought for the personal use of the buyer or for investment purposes. A shoe store owner can buy a building to use as a new location for their store. They'd be called an amenity buyer. However, you could buy the same property and rent it to the shoe store owner, and you'd be an investor. That said, there are some properties that *only* fit the investment model. For example, take a 100-unit apartment building. You may buy it to live in one of the apartments, but its ability to generate income is much more important than providing one unit for you to live in.

**How it is used:** I told my broker to find me another **investment property** to add to my portfolio.

## location analysis

a study of a geographical area

**What it is:** real estate investors studying a general space/region to determine if it's a good place to invest

**How it works:** Some real estate investors examine a general geographic area to determine if it's a good location for a particular type of investment. For example, someone wanting to invest in a large warehouse-type retail store will study the area for the nearest competition, highway access, need for the store, and area to be served. If a property meets most or all of these requirements, the location analysis indicates it's a successful space to invest. Ultimately, the idea is to determine if the area can support the intended investment.

**How it is used:** The buyer asked the staff to prepare a **location analysis** to see if there could be a need for a new movie theater.

## market research

obtaining information about the real estate market

**What it is:** a study of all the aspects of the real estate market to guide investment decisions

**How it works:** Market research is a blanket term for the many studies that can be done to determine the possible success of a real estate investment.

While predicting the future is impossible, a study of current conditions may help in deciding on whether to invest in property. The neighborhood and location analysis discussed in this chapter are part of market research. The goals of the investor and the potential of the investment to meet those goals may also be part of a market study. Any information that will help the investor decide could be considered part of market research.

**How it is used:** The investor's **market research** showed not much demand for the type of building they wanted to buy.

## neighborhood analysis
### determining if the specific area is right for the investment

**What it is:** a study of how well the project fits in a given local area

**How it works:** Every real estate investment type has its own requirements with respect to the neighborhood in which it's located. Commercial properties need public transportation, road access, parking, and supporting businesses like restaurants. Residential properties need grocery stores and schools. Industrial properties need highway access and buffer areas. A neighborhood analysis provides information on how well the neighborhood will support the investment.

**How it is used:** The **neighborhood analysis** indicated that the neighborhood could support an apartment building rather than an office building.

## property condition
### the physical construction and maintenance status of the property

**What it is:** an issue when selecting an improved property (one with a building on it), this is both the original quality of the construction and how it's been maintained/upgraded during its lifetime

**How it works:** The day an investor buys a property, all the benefits and problems associated with that property become the investor's responsibility. This includes any physical problems with the land or building, such as faulty wiring or plumbing. A thorough inspection of the building and property should be done by a professionally certified inspector or engineer prior to purchasing the property. Newly constructed buildings should also be inspected for the quality of construction as well as compliance with all government codes (regulations set by the governing body).

**How it is used:** Before the couple made an offer, they wanted to have a full **property condition** inspection completed.

## reciprocal agreement

a consensus between two or more property owners

**What it is:** an understanding between property owners guaranteeing certain rights and obligations with respect to each other

**How it works:** Reciprocal agreements are used when the individual property owners wish to cooperate to develop their properties but require certain rights from each other. For example, several property owners wishing to build a shopping mall would need guaranteed permission for shared driveways, parking, and common area use from each other. A shared driveway between two homeowners is often a reciprocal agreement. One person uses their owned portion and gives the other the right to use it (easement), and vice versa.

**How it is used:** The four property owners wishing to retain ownership of their individual properties decided that a **reciprocal agreement** would take care of the issues that would occur when they built the office complex together.

## risk assessment

evaluating the potential that a real estate investment is not successful

**What it is:** the act of studying the various ways an investment may not be successful in achieving an investor's goals

**How it works:** An investor generally wants to make a steady amount of money on their investment. The investor may have a specific goal with respect to how profitable their investment should be, and they will then assess the investment's level of risk alongside their investment goals. The investor will also factor in how much risk they can personally stand. For example, if the property begins losing money, how long can the investor use their own funds to pay the property's bills? Ultimately, it's an exercise of trying to determine whether the risk is worth the potential gain and how to minimize risk and ensure gain.

**How it is used:** After doing a **risk assessment**, the investor decided that they could afford a year of losing money before they'd be forced to sell at a loss.

## tenant demand

### the amount and kind of space renters want

**What it is:** the number of tenants willing to rent is a crucial factor in selecting an investment rental property; the more tenants who want to rent, the more profitable the investment

**How it works:** The ideal situation is for an investor to own a building with many people wanting to rent the space in that building—this is a high tenant demand. The two factors in determining tenant demand are the type of space offered and the potential renters' desire or need. For example, most apartments have two or fewer bedrooms. People who need three bedrooms often prefer a house. A building with all three-bedroom apartments might be a bad investment. Another example of low tenant demand would be office tenants who are looking for spaces of less than 1,000 square feet, and your building only offers 5,000-square-foot rentals.

**How it is used:** Based on **tenant demand**, the office building owner decided to divide up each 10,000-square-foot floor into smaller spaces.

## vacancy rate

### a measure of available rental space

**What it is:** the mathematical relationship between all rental space and available rental space

**How it works:** To determine the vacancy rate, first pick the type of space you want to measure and designate the building, complex, neighborhood, or area you want to measure. Then, you'll need to get two numbers: the total amount of that kind of space in that building or area and the total amount of vacant space in that building or area. By dividing the vacant space by the total space, you find the vacancy rate. Say you have a 100,000-square-foot office building and 10,000 square feet of that building are not rented. The vacancy rate for the building is 10% because 10,000 ÷ 100,000 = 10%. For communities like towns and cities, the vacancy rate numbers are often publicly available.

**How it is used:** We needed to calculate the area's commercial office space **vacancy rate** before proceeding with the purchase of the building.

## vacancy rate analysis

### calculating and studying the vacancy rate

**What it is:** the vacancy rate (the amount of unrented space related to total space) can be examined to provide information regarding rent levels, marketing, and investment strategy

**How it works:** Studying the vacancy rate of a building or area may reveal a lot about that space, for good or bad. A persistent high vacancy rate of a certain type of space might indicate a permanent change in the market for that space. On the other hand, a temporary high vacancy rate might be due to a change in the normal business cycle or rents that are too high. A low vacancy rate, say 5%, in a residential apartment building, generally indicates that rents could be raised.

**How it is used:** The **vacancy rate analysis** showed a 30% vacancy rate for retail space in the town, possibly due to more online shopping.

## walkability index

### a way to measure how convenient it is to get around without a vehicle in a neighborhood

**What it is:** a system using numbers to rate how easy it is to do routine tasks on foot—the more walkable a neighborhood, the higher the score

**How it works:** The walkability of a neighborhood may impact its value to those looking to buy there. Some areas, like downtowns that may have a mix of business, stores, and residents, will be very walkable. A person might be able to get their dry cleaning, go food shopping, and stop at the library all on foot. In suburban areas that are automobile dependent, a person might only be able to walk a little at each shopping center that they visit. This kind of an area would get a low score. The US Environmental Protection Agency developed the walkability index.

**How it is used:** The area had a high **walkability index**, making it a good spot for an investment in an apartment building.

# CHAPTER 3

# Financing

Real estate is generally expensive to invest in. If you had to save the total amount of money to buy an investment property or even a house to live in, you might never get there. The price of the property may increase faster than the amount of money you could save to buy it.

Consequently, an entire industry has developed around borrowing money to buy your own home as well as investment properties. Private industry, through banks and other organizations that lend money directly, serves the consumer. These organizations are sometimes called retail lenders. The federal government has also designed programs to help the consumer as well as the lenders.

While borrowing money to buy real estate can be risky, it also allows the buyer to purchase property they could otherwise not afford. Reducing the amount of buyers' money involved in a purchase can also create the possibility of increased profits.

In this chapter, you'll get a basic understanding of the terminology used in real estate financing. After absorbing these terms, you'll be more comfortable talking with brokers and other financial experts who can help you buy your first, or twenty-first, real estate investment.

## amortized loan

**What it is:** a loan requiring that you make payments on the principal and interest during the term (amount of time) of the loan

**How it works:** A typical home mortgage loan is an amortized loan. The loan requires monthly payments that include the interest owed and a portion of the principal (the amount borrowed). The payments are fixed to be the same each month. Interest is calculated on the remaining balance of what is owed. This means that over time, the amount of interest decreases, and the amount of principal paid increases each month. The loan is fully paid at the end of the term. Another name for an amortized loan is a direct reduction loan.

**How it is used:** The thirty-year **amortized loan** we got to buy the house means we'll owe nothing after the last payment.

## ARM (adjustable rate mortgage)

**What it is:** when a loan is made, the interest rate (percentage fee for borrowing) can change over time, resulting in changing payments

**How it works:** An adjustable rate mortgage (ARM) allows the borrower to share the lender's risk that overall interest rates in the economy will go up or down. Because of this, the advantage to the borrower is that the initial interest rate will usually be lower than with a fixed rate mortgage (where the interest rate charged stays the same the entire duration of the loan). These ARM loans generally have a set period when the interest rate will be recalculated for the following year's payments.

**How it is used:** I'll be getting a raise before the first adjustment period on the **ARM**, so we should be fine if the payments go up.

## bridge loan

**What it is:** a short-lived financing arrangement, also called interim financing, temporary loan, swing loan, or gap loan

**How it works:** A bridge loan is typically used to get past a situation where someone may be selling a property and buying another property at the same time. They may need the money from the sale to go ahead with the purchase but can't get the dates to work out. A bridge loan to buy the new property, to be repaid as soon as the old property is sold, may be used to deal with this issue. The lender may want some assurance, like a signed sales contract that the old property will be sold in a short time.

**How it is used:** Since the closing of their old house was postponed, they'll have to get a **bridge loan** to buy the new house before they lose it to another buyer.

## closing costs

### the money paid when property ownership is transferred

**What it is:** the various charges paid at the time of finishing up the purchase of a property, which is the time ownership is transferred

**How it works:** When title is transferred, during the closing process, especially if there is a mortgage loan involved, there are a number of charges and credits to the buyer and seller. These will be listed in a closing statement and are expected to be settled at the closing. These charges could be anything from taxes owed on the property to leftover fuel oil in the property's heating system. If everything is not resolved, the sale may not go through.

**How it is used:** The buyer was glad to be alerted to the **closing costs**, which were more than expected.

## conventional loan

### a mortgage loan that meets certain conditions

**What it is:** loans that meet criteria or conditions set by lenders and often by the secondary market

**How it works:** To standardize most mortgage loans, lenders as well as the secondary market (where lenders sell mortgage debt) create various standards and conditions that these loans have to meet. These criteria could be the minimum amount of a down payment, a minimum credit score, and the financial status of the borrowers' other debts. If the loan meets all conditions demanded, it is deemed a conventional loan. At the federal level, the criteria for conventional mortgage loans can change from time to time as a result of market conditions, government regulations, and credit risk trends. Local lenders can also change their criteria based on local market conditions and risk factors.

**How it is used:** The easiest thing to do is apply for a **conventional loan** for our mortgage.

## debt service

### the periodic payment for the loan

**What it is:** the technical term for what a homeowner calls their mortgage payment, which is usually made on a monthly basis

**How it works:** All real estate loans must be paid off, but how you do it depends on the specifics of the lender's agreement at the time the loan was made. The typical repayment plan, and the one most often used for homeowners, is a payment of a portion of principal and interest every month until the loan is paid in full. In many cases, the lender will require the borrower to include a portion of their annual property taxes and homeowners' insurance premiums (both of which will then be paid by the lender) as part of the monthly mortgage payment. These payments are not part of the debt service. Debt service (the mortgage payment) includes only principal and interest payment.

**How it is used:** Increasing the loan amount will increase the **debt service** but will allow for a lower down payment.

## DTI (debt-to-income) ratio

### how much debt a person has relative to their income

**What it is:** a measurement that creditors use to determine the ability of a borrower to pay back the loan (or, using real estate terms, the mortgage)

**How it works:** The debt-to-income (DTI) ratio is a calculation done by dividing the total monthly debt payments by the total monthly gross income. For example, if a person pays $1,000 per month in a combination of credit card bills and a car loan, and their gross monthly salary is $5,000, their DTI ratio is 20%. Say the bank's maximum allowable DTI ratio is 40%. The bank could then approve a loan, where the payments of which would bring the individual's DTI ratio up to 40% of their gross monthly income. Different lenders will use different levels of DTI to approve a loan.

**How it is used:** Fortunately, the bank was using a 36% **DTI ratio**, and the couple's DTI ratio was only 20%.

## equity

the amount of a property's value that you own

**What it is:** the difference between the debt owed on the property and the market value (a value without limitations) of the property

**How it works:** Equity is the portion of the fair market sale price the seller would walk away with if the property were sold. The value of the property, as well as debts owed on the property, will change over time, resulting in a change in the equity in the property. Many properties have mortgage loans, and payments are then made against those loans. Property values may increase over time due to market conditions, or improvements may be made that increase the value of the property. In addition, some owners may take out loans against their property's value for one reason or another. All these can result in a change in the equity.

**How it is used:** The market value of the property was $800,000 and the owner still owed $500,000 on the mortgage, making their **equity** $300,000.

## equity financing

a way to raise money

**What it is:** creating financial success by selling shares in a business; real estate investors can make use of this concept even though the term applies to any business, not just real estate investment

**How it works:** *Equity* means the financial interest that is actually or will be owned, not financed, by lender money. Say someone who owns a piece of property outright (or without a mortgage) wants to raise money to build a structure on their land. This owner may then decide to sell shares in ownership of the property instead of borrowing against the property from a bank; this is an example of equity financing.

**How it is used:** Interest rates, availability of funds to borrow, and the financial status of the owner will determine which option, **equity financing** or lender financing, is better for the borrower.

## escrow account

money collected above the mortgage payment to pay property bills

**What it is:** any account used to temporarily hold money for something that will happen later

**How it works:** In the case of a mortgage loan, the lender wants to make sure the property is protected from foreclosure by the government and from any damage that may occur. As part of the mortgage loan agreement, they will establish an escrow account that the borrower will pay into each month, which will be managed by the loan servicing company handling the ongoing management of the loan. Periodically, the company will pay local property taxes and insurance payments. This type of escrow account may also be called an impound account. The term *escrow* is also used in a slightly different sense related to a way of transferring property ownership, referred to as "closing in escrow."

**How it is used:** The property owner found it easier to pay into the **escrow account** each month instead of keeping track of insurance and tax bills.

## fixed rate mortgage

the interest rate on the mortgage does not change

**What it is:** a loan in which the money that is borrowed is paid back at the same interest rate throughout the lifetime (term) of said loan

**How it works:** With respect to interest rates on mortgage loans, there are basically two options: fixed rate and adjustable rate (adjustable rates mean that the rate can change throughout the term of the loan). In a fixed rate mortgage, the interest rate is stated when the loan is approved and does not change for the entire term of the loan. This means the payment will not change over the loan term. In the adjustable rate mortgage (ARM), the interest rate and therefore the payment amount will change during the loan term.

**How it is used:** The taxes and insurance costs on the property may change, but with a **fixed rate mortgage**, at least the monthly payments won't change.

## foreclosure

the process of someone taking over your property

**What it is:** the legal process where someone can take over ownership of your property against your will because of unpaid debts

**How it works:** The two principal ongoing debts a property owner must pay are the mortgage loan and real estate taxes. The lender and the local municipality have the right to foreclose on a person's property if either of these bills are not paid. Foreclosure proceedings involve notices, grace periods, and time frames for payment in both mortgage loan cases and nonpayment of taxes. A person whose property is subject to foreclosure should seek counsel from an attorney.

**How it is used:** The bank was about to begin **foreclosure** proceedings when the owners came up with the money to make the unpaid mortgage loan payments.

## government-insured loan

a loan that has government guarantees

**What it is:** the federal government has made it easier for people to buy houses through this federal insurance program

**How it works:** The risk a lender takes in providing money through a mortgage loan is that the borrower will be unable to pay off the loan. The federal government has created programs through the Veterans Administration (VA) and the Federal Housing Administration (FHA) that provide insurance to the lender on behalf of the buyer. In the event the buyer can't pay the loan, the government may step in to create repayment plans. Because of the added security that the lender has, the terms of the loan may be more generous, such as a zero (no money down) down payment.

**How it is used:** If the buyer uses a **government-insured loan** program, they might be able to buy the house even if they have no money for the down payment.

# HELOC (home equity line of credit)

**a way to take money out of the portion of the home's value that is actually owned by the homeowner (equity)**

**What it is:** a type of credit allowing the homeowner to withdraw some of the cash value, or equity, of their home

**How it works:** A home equity line of credit (HELOC) is a way for the property owner to borrow from themselves by reducing the equity in their property. Say someone had a home worth $300,000 without a mortgage, and they then took out $100,000 through a HELOC. Assuming the homeowner happened to sell their home before they had made any HELOC payments, they would only net $200,000 from the sale with $100,000 going to the lender to pay off the HELOC. A HELOC is generally used as a line of credit rather than a single lump sum payment to the homeowner borrower. The lenders have different repayment plans, and the money can be used for any purpose.

**How it is used:** The homeowner took out a **HELOC** to fund their child's college education.

## interest-only loan

**a way to reduce the monthly payments during the term of the loan**

**What is it:** a loan where only interest payments are required during the loan's term

**How it works:** During the term of an interest-only loan, the borrower is allowed to make interest payments only. An interest-only loan is different than an amortized loan, where the principal (the amount borrowed) and interest are paid simultaneously. Depending on the agreement, at the end of the term, the borrower may be required to pay the loan off in one lump sum or via a series of payments (which could be higher than the interest-only payments), or they may be able to refinance the loan. Someone may opt to use an interest-only loan to keep their monthly payments low for business or personal finance reasons.

**How it is used:** The **interest-only loan** to buy the property will keep the monthly payments lower so we'll have some extra cash for the business.

## interest rate

### what you pay a lender for use of their money

**What it is:** a percentage paid to a lender to borrow their money

**How it works:** A lender is anyone who lets someone else use their money for a time. A bank might issue a thirty-year home loan. The bank wants its original loan money back plus payment for allowing the use of that money. When you put money in a savings account, you are lending the bank your money as they can then lend it out as a home loan. You expect to be paid something for allowing the bank to make money with your money. The interest rate is the percentage paid to the lender—or in this case, you, the depositor. Unless otherwise noted, interest rates are always stated annually.

**How it is used:** The **interest rate** on the mortgage loan was 5%.

## loan servicing

### the ongoing management of a mortgage loan

**What it is:** the various administrative tasks associated with receiving mortgage payments from the borrower; the lender and the mortgage servicing agency may or may not be the same organization

**How it works:** After a mortgage loan is approved, it is crucial that payments from the borrower are tracked and certain disbursements (payments out) are made. A mortgage servicing agency will typically receive the payments, ensure taxes and insurance escrow accounts (any account used to temporarily hold money) are sufficient, make payments to taxing authorities and insurance companies, and make payments to lenders or other shareholders having a financial interest in the mortgage loan. Borrowers must be notified of any change in their loan servicing company.

**How it is used:** My **loan servicing** company has changed three times.

## LTV (loan-to-value) ratio

### the amount borrowed as a percentage of the property's value

**What it is:** a lender will allow a customer to borrow a percentage of a property's value or sale price; this is a common way to state that as a percentage

**How it works:** Loan-to-value (LTV) ratios are set based on various factors, mostly involving the risk a lender is willing to take on certain properties. However, a lender who normally approves loans of 80% of value might only approve a loan of 60% of value if that's all they estimated a borrower could repay. The LTV ratio is calculated by dividing the loan amount by the value of the property. The amount that will be lent is calculated by multiplying the total value of the property by the LTV ratio.

**How it is used:** The bank uses an 80% **LTV ratio** for single-family homes, so that means they're willing to lend us $400,000 on that $500,000 property.

## mortgage

**using the property as security for the loan**

**What it is:** the document that guarantees the lenders the right to claim ownership of the property if the loan is not paid

**How it works:** When someone borrows money to buy a piece of real estate, it's normal for the lender to ask for the property to be security for the loan. A value is estimated for the property, the borrower's ability to pay is examined, and the loan is made. The borrower is required to sign a document that uses the property as the loan guarantee and allows the lender to take the property if the terms of the loan are not fulfilled. The terms *mortgagor* and *mortgagee* are often confused because the mortgage document is related to the loan of money. The bank is the lender and mortgagee. The buyer is the borrower and mortgagor. The borrower gives the bank a mortgage, which entitles the bank to take the property in the event of a default on the loan.

**How it is used:** Heather had to borrow money from the bank and give them a **mortgage** in order to buy her first home.

## origination fee

**money paid to the lender for mortgage loan processing**

**What it is:** a sum paid to the lender at the beginning of the mortgage loan process to cover the costs of processing the application for the loan

**How it works:** The lender wants all costs for the mortgage loan to be paid by the borrower. One of those costs involves the various tasks that are part of processing a mortgage loan. Different lenders not only charge varying origination fees, but they will also put different charges under the origination fee umbrella. Origination fees must be disclosed to the borrower, and a lender will typically charge a small percentage of the loan amount as an origination fee. Despite its name, this is not an application fee, which is usually a flat fee amount to get the process started.

**How it is used:** I double-checked the closing document to see if the **origination fee** and the other processing fees were accurate.

## PMI (private mortgage insurance)

being insured against not paying the mortgage loan

**What it is:** insurance that the borrower buys to persuade the bank to lend them more than the conventional amount

**How it works:** Banks and the secondary mortgage market have criteria regarding the loan-to-value (LTV) ratio of a mortgage loan. If a buyer wants to borrow a larger amount, there is greater risk to the lender. The lender may require the borrower to take out private mortgage insurance (PMI) to protect the lender against the possibility that the borrower will fail to pay. Say the lender's criteria is to lend 80% of the value of the property and the borrower wants to borrower 95%. The lender might agree if the borrower buys PMI.

**How it is used:** The bank is requiring **PMI**, but it's worth it to not have to save up the larger down payment that would otherwise be needed.

## points

percentage calculated against the mortgage loan amount

**What it is:** lenders use these calculated percentages for various purposes related to the mortgage loan process; as a percentage of the loan, it is a way to relate certain charges to the loan amount

**How it works:** Lenders use points, where one point equates to 1% of the mortgage loan amount, for various reasons. For example, the origination fee (bundled lender fees) might be calculated in points. The lender could charge one or more points as prepaid interest, reducing the original mortgage loan interest rate. If there is a delay between mortgage loan approval and closing, the lender may agree to hold the interest rate until closing for a fee that may be calculated using points—this could be beneficial if interest rates are rising rapidly.

**How it is used:** The bank decided to charge two **points** to lower the original interest rate on the mortgage loan.

## portfolio lender
### a creditor who keeps the loans they make

**What it is:** someone who makes mortgage loans and then retains them as an investment

**How it works:** Most mortgage lenders make mortgage loans and then sell them to other investors or on the secondary market to recoup funds to lend again. Portfolio lenders, which can be banks, credit unions, or other investors, make the loans and then retain them as an investment, receiving money on the interest charged for the loan. Since these loans are not sold to others like on the secondary market, they may not have to meet specific requirements of that market, making the qualification terms sometimes more flexible. However, protections provided by these terms may also not be available.

**How it is used:** The buyer's credit was not as good as it might have been, so they shopped for a mortgage loan from a **portfolio lender**, hoping to get more flexible terms.

## prepayment penalty
### a fee charged by the lender for paying off a loan early

**What it is:** lenders will sometimes charge a fee for paying off a long-term loan, like a mortgage loan, before its final payment is due

**How it works:** When a lender makes a long-term loan, such as a mortgage loan, they expect to get a certain amount of money back (interest) as their return on the investment. Suppose someone comes into some money and decides to pay off the loan right away—the lender will lose their anticipated interest. Most of the interest on amortized mortgage loans is paid in the early years, so prepayment penalties often only apply to a few years at the beginning of the loan. There are federal and state regulations that can affect prepayment penalties. These regulations range from prohibiting them altogether to limiting the number of years (usually 1–3) that they can be in effect. Prepayment penalties can be a fixed percentage of the amount prepaid (the most common method), a flat fee, or a sliding scale of percentages.

**How it is used:** The **prepayment penalty** in their state was 3% of the prepayment amount the first year, 2% the second year, and 1% the third year.

## purchase money mortgage
### a loan used to buy real estate

**What it is:** this term is often used to describe a mortgage loan made by the seller of a property, either as the buyer's first mortgage loan or a second (supplemental) loan; technically, this can be any mortgage used as security for a property loan

**How it works:** For various financial reasons, sometimes a seller is willing to take a small or no down payment when selling a property. The seller is not actually lending the buyer any money but is extending credit. The seller gets little or no money up front and gets paid over a period of time, often years, for the amount of credit that has been extended. If this is the only financing for the purchase, it may also be known as seller financing. At other times, the buyer might borrow as much as they can from a lender and then borrow all or most of the remaining balance from the seller giving a second mortgage to the seller as security for the amount of credit the seller is extending.

**How it is used:** After we got the mortgage loan from the bank for most of the purchase price, the seller offered us a **purchase money mortgage** to cover the down payment.

## refinance
### taking out a new loan on existing property

**What it is:** getting a new mortgage loan on property the investor already owns

**How it works:** An owner can refinance, that is, take out a new mortgage loan replacing the old one, on mortgaged property they already own or take out a new mortgage on a property that has no mortgage in order to get a lump sum of cash. There are many reasons that someone would do this. For example, interest rates may have gone down from the time of the original loan, so refinancing will reduce debt service payments. Or, perhaps, the owner may want to take out some of the property's equity (the amount of a property's value that is not subject to be repaid to the lender) for repairs or to invest in something else.

**How it is used:** Interest rates had gone down two points, so it made sense to **refinance** the original mortgage loan.

## REIT (real estate investment trust)

a way to invest in real estate without owning property

**What it is:** a company that invests in real estate in various ways, for example, buying, selling, managing, and financing large-scale projects

**How it works:** A real estate investment trust (REIT) allows investors to buy shares in a real estate investing company. The advantage of a REIT is that it allows individuals to invest in the real estate market without actually owning or managing property. Like all investments in stock, it has risks associated with it. There are three types of REITs: an equity REIT invests in properties, a mortgage REIT buys debt as an investment, and a hybrid or combination REIT invests in both properties and debt.

**How it is used:** The investor did not want to directly own investment properties, so they bought shares in a **REIT**.

## second mortgage

an additional mortgage loan on the property

**What it is:** if a buyer or an existing owner already has a mortgage loan on the property, this is another mortgage loan against the property without paying off the original (first) mortgage loan

**How it works:** Depending on the order of the mortgage loans or other agreements, the first mortgage loan is the first one to be paid in the event of a foreclosure. The second mortgage loan holder would be the next in line to be paid, and so on. A third mortgage loan is possible, as well. Second mortgages are sometimes used to take money out of the property if the equity (the amount of a property's value that you own above and beyond the remaining balance of the mortgage loan) has increased.

**How it is used:** They needed a lump sum of cash to buy the vacation home they wanted, so they took out a **second mortgage** loan on their home.

## secondary market

government-sponsored enterprises that buy mortgage debt

**What it is:** a place where lenders can exchange (sell) their mortgage loans for cash to make more loans

**How it works:** Say a bank has a million dollars to lend out in mortgage loans. When it's lent out all of that money, how will it make new loans? The bank will sell some mortgage loans to government-supported financial companies like Fannie Mae and Ginnie Mae and receive cash that they can then lend out. This secondary selling of a mortgage debt to these government-sponsored corporations is performed on the secondary market. Because of the financial risk in buying mortgage loans, the secondary market can also set the terms for conventional loans.

**How it is used:** The banker explained to the borrower that they had no choice but to follow **secondary market** guidelines when making mortgage loans.

## seller financing

a seller extends credit to the buyer in order to help them purchase the seller's property

**What it is:** a situation where the seller, through a mortgage loan, is willing to help the buyer buy the property

**How it works:** Seller financing may occur when the buyer's credit negatively affects their ability to obtain a regular mortgage loan. It may also occur when the buyer's approval plus their cash still does not equal the purchase price. Seller financing is sometimes used to provide the buyers with a more favorable loan rate when mortgage loan rates are high, and it's sometimes referred to as a purchase money mortgage. The seller financing works when the seller agrees to take less cash at the closing and chooses to receive payments over time with interest. These private transactions are kept between the buyer and seller. The credit is secured with a note that reflects the buyer's signed promise to pay. The buyer also gives a mortgage to the seller, allowing the seller to foreclose and take possession of the property if the buyer defaults on the money owed.

**How it is used:** The seller offered to provide **seller financing** for a portion of the price.

## short sale

a distress sale of property by the owner

**What it is:** a sale of property by the owner for less than the mortgage loan amount with the approval of the lender

**How it works:** In a down-turning real estate market, sometimes a property ends up being worth less than the remaining balance on the mortgage loan (underwater). If the lender agrees, the owner is allowed to sell the property for the lesser amount, which is turned over to the bank. Sometimes the lender will forgive the rest of the loan, or they may try to get payment from other assets the borrower may have. A short sale will usually have to be justified by multiple appraisals and time on the market to prove that the property is worth what the owners claim it to be.

**How it is used:** The bank agreed to a **short sale** after the property was on the market for ten months and two appraisals confirmed the lower value of the property.

# CHAPTER 4

# Property Management

On the day you take ownership of your investment property, you're responsible for everything about the property, including the furnace that breaks down that night. The point is, way before closing day, you, the owner, need to have a management plan in place. You can manage the property yourself, hire a professional, or do some combination of those two. No matter which option you choose, as the owner, you are still responsible.

This chapter provides terms that cover any of the three roads you take in regard to property management. Almost *all* the terms will apply if you decide to self-manage as what is usually called the "landlord." Most of these terms will help you understand and interact with the professional manager if you hire one. The terms will also be important in understanding what responsibilities you may want to take on in a hybrid management model.

Many people want to own investment property. Many do not want to be landlords, or hands-on managers. So, the terms in this chapter should introduce you to the management side of owning an investment property, helping you make the right choice about management. You may find it's worth handling your property yourself, after all.

Note that the terms *landlord* and *manager* are used somewhat interchangeably throughout this chapter, since either will be responsible for day-to-day operations.

## actual eviction

kicking out a tenant from a rented unit against their will

**What it is:** the legal process of removing a tenant from a rented building or space for legal cause

**How it works:** Occasionally, a tenant must be removed from occupying their space or unit in a building or on a property. Some of the causes that might result in eviction are nonpayment of rent, doing damage to the property, interfering in other tenants' peaceful enjoyment of the property, or other violations of the lease terms. Eviction is a legal proceeding that takes place in court or other court-like administrative settings. Eviction proceedings are initiated by the property owner or property manager. This person may or may not be represented by an attorney.

**How it is used:** After the tenant had missed three months of rent payments, the owner began **actual eviction** proceedings.

## asset manager

someone who handles the investment aspects of one or more properties

**What it is:** a person responsible for maintaining and increasing the investment value of the properties under their supervision

**How it works:** The job of an asset manager can best be understood in contrast to the job of a property manager. An asset manager looks at the investment and profitability aspects of property in advising owners and making decisions on their behalf, while a property manager handles the day-to-day operations of the property. The asset manager will rely on the property manager not only to maintain the property, but to provide accurate financial and maintenance reports about the property. These reports can then be considered in the asset manager's investment decisions about the property.

**How it is used:** The **asset manager** asked the property manager to send them next year's projected budget to see if the building's profitability was in line with the owner's investment goals.

## capital budget

**a financial look ahead at large repair or improvement items for a property**

**What it is:** a projection of expenses for items that may need replacement or for property improvement projects

**How it works:** Capital budget items occur once, like building a swimming pool, or occur on a long-term basis, like installing a new roof every so many years. Capital budget items are not annually recurring expenses. A capital budget is used to plan for these generally large cost items. An owner or manager might set aside money ahead of time to take care of the items when needed, or the owner may borrow money for a specific project if that is more feasible.

**How it is used:** The manager worked with the owner to decide how to fund the **capital budget**.

## constructive eviction

**actions taken by the owner that make the building unable to be lived in (uninhabitable)**

**What it is:** an illegal way to try to get tenants to leave the building

**How it works:** Sometimes an owner decides not to go through the legal system to evict a tenant. They will resort to such activities as turning off the heat, not doing repairs for a significant length of time, and generally harassing tenants. The idea behind the term is that the owner is creating (constructing) a situation that makes the building unsuitable, or even impossible, to live in. All such activities are illegal and may even be dangerous to the tenants.

**How it is used:** The tenants sued the owner on the grounds that the actions were **constructive eviction** to make them move.

## fair housing laws

**laws that prohibit discrimination in housing**

**What it is:** laws passed by the federal, state, and local governments to prevent discrimination in the sale and rental of housing

**How it works:** Discrimination in the sale and rental of housing has been addressed at all levels of government with the establishment of fair housing laws. Federal laws apply to everyone, state laws apply to properties within the state, and local laws apply to properties within that municipality (city or town). The two things landlords and property managers should be aware of are: actions that the landlord may not take and the protected classes that the laws cover. Landlords are responsible to know and follow whatever laws apply to their properties, including fair employment laws, if they hire someone to help them manage the property.

**How it is used:** The fines for violating **fair housing laws** can be quite large.

## financial accounting

### tracking all monetary transactions

**What it is:** a system established to account for and track all economic matters related to the investment property

**How it works:** Tracking finances and maintaining financial records is critical to owning and managing an investment property. Financial accounting includes tracking tax issues, monitoring capital gains issues, refinancing, and calculating profit and loss statements; all of which depends on maintaining accurate records of income and expenses. Common accounting software as well as software aimed at real estate management are available and may be useful if looking for a DIY approach. However, an accountant with real estate experience is an asset, especially when self-managing property.

**How it is used:** All the records from the owner's **financial accounting** came in handy during the IRS audits.

## financial reporting

### a regular report completed by the property manager to the owner

**What it is:** an accounting report done by the professional manager on a regular basis and sent to keep the owner informed of the status of the building

**How it works:** The financial report is usually provided to the owner monthly. The content and frequency of the report will have been agreed to in the management agreement. Although it's called a financial report, it will likely have additional information. So, in addition to the status of the property's financial accounts, the report may include information about upcoming lease expirations, the amount of currently unoccupied space, projects that have been completed since the last report, and a projection of upcoming projects.

**How it is used:** The owner and the manager agreed that the monthly **financial reporting** should be supplemented with additional quarterly reporting about the building's maintenance issues.

## government code
### law passed by the government

**What it is:** technically any law passed by the government can be called a code, ordinance, or regulation; this book obviously focuses on ones pertaining to real estate

**How it works:** There are many codes or laws that can affect a real estate investment. Some have to do with physical land, others relate directly to buildings on the property, and still others have to do with the landlord-tenant relationship. An example of these government codes is the zoning ordinance, which governs how property is developed and used. The building, plumbing, and electrical governmental codes provide the minimum standards for building construction. Additionally, it's common for local and state governments to pass tenant-protection laws. These laws may deal with issues like the amount of security a landlord may collect and the minimum notice required for a rent increase.

**How it is used:** A landlord must be familiar with and comply with all applicable **government codes**.

## hybrid (combination) property management
### a combination of self-management and professional management

**What it is:** using a combination of self-management and outside management to reduce the burden on the owner and reduce the cost of using only professional management

**How it works:** A property owner may wish to manage an investment property themselves, but they may not have the time. Conversely, the property may not generate enough money to hire a full-time professional manager. Some choose to divide tasks between the owner and an outside staff member. For example, suppose the investment property is quite a distance from the owner's home. The owner might hire someone from the neighborhood or give someone in the building a rent discount to handle any emergencies that come up. Likewise, an owner might hire a management company to handle day-to-day issues in the building but retain rent collection and lease negotiations themselves. The hybrid decision, like the self-management decision, is often influenced by the experience of the owner.

**How it is used:** The property management company offered several levels of service for owners who wanted a **hybrid property management** arrangement.

## kickback

**a secret, unauthorized payment made at someone else's expense**

**What it is:** usually when someone demands payment for favorable treatment where a third party is paying for the service

**How it works:** A kickback happens when someone, representing a third party, demands a secret payment from someone they've hired as payment for giving them the job. For example, a management company hires a cleaning company for the building. In consideration of awarding the cleaning company the contract, which the owner is paying for out of the building's proceeds, the management company demands payment from the cleaning company of 10% of the contract fee. This is an unauthorized payment to the management company which the owner is ultimately paying for. Kickbacks are always unethical, illegal, and/or a violation of state regulations.

**How it is used:** The owner caught the management company in an illegal **kickback** scheme.

## leasing consultant

**someone who helps find tenants**

**What it is:** a real estate professional hired to focus on finding tenants and negotiating with them on behalf of the landlord

**How it works:** One of the more difficult and specialized aspects of owning an investment property, especially a commercial property, is finding suitable tenants and negotiating lease terms. This is where a leasing consultant comes in—these professionals are usually licensed brokers or salespersons aimed at helping the leasing process. These professionals may represent the landlord or the tenant and may be paid by either, depending on the agreement and common practice in the area.

**How it is used:** The landlord managed the everyday operations of the building, but they hired a real estate broker to act as a **leasing consultant** to find tenants and negotiate leases.

## liability

### assignment of blame

**What it is:** a legal term that means someone is held responsible for something negative that happens

**How it works:** Though not a legal definition, for purposes of this book, liability means the assignment of responsibility should something bad happen. For example, someone slips on an icy sidewalk outside of a large apartment building, and it's determined that the landlord should have shoveled the snow. Liability is assigned to the landlord, who may have to financially compensate the injured person. Liability is the reason risk management is an important aspect of property management.

**How it is used:** The court determined that the owner had **liability** for the blocked fire door that caused the tenant to be injured in the fire.

## lien

### financial obligation against the property

**What it is:** a monetary obligation placed against the property due to an unpaid bill by the owner

**How it works:** A lien is a way to ensure that someone hired to do work to a property is paid. Say a plumber does some work on a property, and the owner fails to pay the plumber's bill. The plumber can file a mechanic's lien with the town or county against the property. When the property is sold, the lien will appear as a cloud (problem) on the title and will need to be paid. If it is not paid, the lien will become an obligation of the new owner because a lien stays with the property rather than the owner. A mortgage loan creates a lien, as do unpaid taxes.

**How it is used:** The title search showed that the property was free of all **liens**.

## local landlord laws

laws governing the legal aspects of the landlord-tenant relationship

**What it is:** the landlord-tenant relationship is a legal one; many state and local governments passed laws governing the obligations of landlords toward the tenants

**How it works:** Landlord laws can be found at the state or local level and vary greatly. They govern things like security deposits, late penalties, and rent increases. In a self-management situation, the landlord must familiarize themselves with the laws so they don't violate them. While these laws can protect both parties, they are primarily designed to protect residential tenants from landlords who might take unfair advantage of people needing a place to live. For example, a law might be passed that requires the landlord to give the tenant three months' notice of a rent increase instead of whatever notice they want to give.

**How it is used:** The **local landlord laws** in that state allow the landlord to ask for only one month's rent as a deposit.

## operating budget

a look ahead at expenses

**What it is:** a one-year projection (look ahead) of all expenses associated with an investment property

**How it works:** An operating budget projects (estimates) all property expenses for a one-year period. This is done for budgeting purposes, to set spending targets, and to estimate the profitability of the property. Previous years' expenses are examined to create realistic projections of future expenses. Management actions may also be considered if they might have an effect on expenses. For example, reducing fuel costs by installing a new heating system or increasing spending on a professional plowing service during the winter by hiring a more reliable plowing company.

**How it is used:** The management company sent the owner an **operating budget** for the following year to get their approval.

## property maintenance

work done to maintain the value and usability of the property

**What it is:** repairs and upkeep of buildings and the equipment in and around those buildings in response to wear and tear from use or time

**How it works:** To maintain the value of a property and to keep it in a useful, desirable state for renters, repair and replacement must be an ongoing process. There are several different kinds of required property maintenance. They come down to preventing problems (preventive maintenance) and fixing problems (corrective maintenance). Landlords should develop a schedule for routine, preventive maintenance. They should also always look for developing issues that need to be corrected before they get worse.

**How it is used:** The buyer did a thorough inspection of the building to develop a plan for **property maintenance** as soon as ownership was transferred.

## property management agreement

the contract between a property owner and a property manager

**What it is:** if an owner chooses to use professional management to manage their investment property, a contractual agreement is signed between the people/groups stating various duties and obligations of the owner and the manager

**How it works:** As in any business arrangement, both parties (the owner and the manager) want to ensure clarity regarding responsibilities of their respective roles. The agreement is primarily a statement of the duties of the manager. The terms of the agreement will cover how long the agreement lasts and the responsibilities, like rent collection, maintenance, and bill paying, that the manager has. The agreement will also state the authority the manager has, for example, to spend a certain amount of money without having to get the owner's permission. The owner will agree to pay the manager a certain amount and may also have responsibility for things like lease approval and rent setting.

**How it is used:** The owner and the manager were very happy with the terms of the **property management agreement**.

## property manager

a person who takes care of all aspects of a property for someone else

**What it is:** a person or company that is hired by a property owner to handle all or most of the aspects of operating the property

**How it works:** Not every investment property owner has the time, skill, or desire to manage their property, especially if they own more than one investment property. There are individuals and companies who can provide skilled management services in these instances; they're referred to as property managers. These professionals generally handle most, or all, of the tasks involved in operating the property. Traditionally, the goal of the manager is to maximize the income from the property while maintaining or increasing the value of the property.

**How it is used:** The new owner did not have time to manage the property day-to-day, so they hired a **property manager**.

## property manager license

government regulation of property managers

**What it is:** a government qualification that assures the public of the competence of a property manager

**How it works:** In order to protect the public, real estate activities have been regulated for a long time. An individual can do things like buying, selling, and renting their own property without a license. Licenses are required for anyone performing certain services for another person with the expectation of being paid for those services.

License laws for real estate management vary by state. Some states include real estate management under normal broker licensing, while others have a separate license for property managers. Depending on the state, if a property manager is licensed under a general real estate broker's license, they may not have significant specialized training in property management. A property owner should check on the licensing status, training, and experience of a manager before hiring.

**How it is used:** Unfortunately, they did not have the appropriate **property manager license**, so I couldn't hire them to manage my building.

## protected class

a group of people covered by antidiscrimination laws

**What it is:** one of the key elements of fair housing and fair employment laws are the groups covered by these laws

**How it works:** The way fair housing and fair employment laws work is to designate certain characteristics that cannot be used as a basis of discrimination. People who fall under these umbrellas are considered protected classes. For example, there are laws in place that prohibit discrimination on the basis of race.

Federal, state, and local laws often have different protected classes. This is not a conflict and should be read cumulatively. A landlord may not discriminate against classes in the federal law, *and* classes in the state law, *and* classes in the local law.

**How it is used:** The landlord consulted with their local human rights commission to make sure they knew what the **protected classes** were in their location.

## rent collection

the system by which the tenant pays their rent

**What it is:** any rental property must have this system to track payments or nonpayments of rents

**How it works:** Whether an investment property is professionally managed or owner managed, it should have a regular rent collection system in place that is understood by all concerned, especially the tenants. The system must include a statement of the rent for each rental unit, the rent due date, and a late payment date after which a defined monetary penalty will be charged. Additionally, it should state how the rent will be collected, for example, sent by mail or paid by electronic means. If the building is professionally managed, the system may include a notification to the owner of nonpayment or chronically late payers or any other information regarding rent collection activities.

**How it is used:** The owner reviewed the responsibilities of **rent collection** with the management company.

## rent roll

### a list of units or space and rent

**What it is:** a table listing the various units (apartments) or space (commercial buildings) and the rents associated with those units or spaces; it's tabulated on an annual basis

**How it works:** In order to make budget projections, an organized estimate of income is necessary. The rent roll is constructed to show total rents for a year for the building. For an apartment building, it would be organized by the number of different kinds of units multiplied by the rents for that unit. So, if the building had 10 one-bedroom units renting at $1,000.00 each and 10 two-bedroom units renting at $2,000.00 each, the rent roll would be: $(10 \times \$1,000 = \$10,000) + (10 \times \$2,000 = \$20,000) = \$30,000$ in monthly rent. To calculate annual rent, you multiply the monthly rent ($30,000) by 12. So, $30,000 \times 12 = \$360,000$ in annual rent.

**How it is used:** It looks like the **rent roll** will cover all the building expenses and the mortgage payment.

## risk management

### dealing with risks of injury to others

**What it is:** the analysis of physical situations that may cause injury to a person; it is an important component of property management

**How it works:** An owner, a professional manager, or a risk professional will inspect the property for possible dangers and suggest ways to deal with those conditions; this is referred to as risk management. Typically, risks might be eliminated, mitigated (made less dangerous), or passed on to another party, through insurance. For example, a swimming pool at a hotel is a risk. Assuming the hotel does not want to eliminate the pool, removing the diving board, having restricted hours, and hiring lifeguards all further reduce the risk. In addition, the hotel can ensure that swimming pool accidents are covered by the hotel's insurance policy. Risk management is examining and acting on all types of risks on the property.

**How it is used:** The new owner was very concerned about **risk management** and discussed it with the new property manager.

## security deposit

money paid to the landlord as insurance

**What it is:** in most leasing situations, the landlord requires a sum of money for incidentals when signing the lease; this deposit is held in a special account by the landlord as insurance against damage that the tenant might do to the property

**How it works:** At lease signing, the landlord usually requires an amount equivalent to one or more months' rent for the security deposit. This money is held until the end of the lease. If there is no damage, the full amount is returned to the tenant. Where permitted and as stated in the lease, the landlord may retain a portion of the deposit for a cleaning fee. Depending on local law, the deposit may or may not be retained for nonpayment of rent. Local laws may limit how much of a deposit can be required. Likewise, landlords have been known to require multiple months' rent up front when signing a lease. This also may be restricted by local law.

**How it is used:** The time frame in which a **security deposit** must be returned to the tenant may be governed by local law.

## service contract

using outside people to perform a certain job

**What it is:** an agreement between the owner/building manager and a company/individual to perform ongoing tasks in the building

**How it works:** Rather than hiring permanent employees to perform certain jobs, building owners or property managers will contract with specialty companies to provide certain services. Let's say cleaning is provided as a service by the landlord in a commercial office building—a cleaning company might be hired to do this job. Managing this contracted work will include making sure the cleaning people show up when they are supposed to and that the quality of service is satisfactory. Unfortunately, when management companies are involved, kickbacks (illegal payments to the management company) are always a concern when dealing with outside contractors.

**How it is used:** The owner told the management company that they didn't care how many **service contracts** the company used as long as the jobs got done and the owner got their monthly check.

## tenant relations

**the overall interaction between management and the tenants**

**What it is:** the relationship between the owner or property manager and the tenants—a good relationship is built on satisfactory facilities/rented space

**How it works:** The goal of owning an investment property is to make money. If all the financial decisions have been correctly made, making money with a rental building, whether residential or commercial, is about getting and keeping good tenants. Tenant relations involve maintaining the building so that complaints are kept to a minimum. Complaints, when made, should then be handled promptly and to the satisfaction of the tenant. Tenants should also be kept informed of all building-related projects to improve the property or that may inconvenience them for a time. Well-managed buildings with high tenant satisfaction get to be well known in an area just as buildings with low tenant satisfaction do.

**How it is used:** The building had a reputation in the area for good **tenant relations**.

## tenant screening

**reviewing tenant applications before renting to them**

**What it is:** the best-run and sometimes the most profitable buildings have a rigorous process for researching the background of someone who wants to rent in their building

**How it works:** Tenant screening requires every applicant for an apartment or space (commercial building) to complete an application form. There is no one standard required form, but generally landlords want to know about the financial status of the applicant, including job history. References from employers or other people may be required, as well as a reference from the previous landlord if available. A credit history will also be most likely required. Landlords must be careful not to ask any questions that would violate fair housing laws.

**How it is used:** The landlord told the applicant that the **tenant screening** process would take several days after they had submitted their application.

## turnover rate

how often tenants move out

**What it is:** a mathematical number representing how often tenants move into and out of the building

**How it works:** The turnover rate is the number of tenants that move out at the end of their leases in proportion to the total number of tenants during that period. So, if 10 tenants moved out last year and you had 100 tenants in the building during that time, the turnover rate is 10%. High turnover can cause a reduction in profits since space or units may be vacant for some time and work may have to be done to rent the unit or space again. Analyzing the turnover rate can be helpful in determining if efforts to retain tenants are successful or what other steps might be taken to reduce turnover.

**How it is used:** Even though the building **turnover rate** was in line with other apartment buildings in the area, the manager wanted to try and reduce it.

# CHAPTER 5

# Leases

A lease is the legal document that establishes and describes a space rental relationship between a landlord and a tenant. Many leases are quite simple, especially those for residential units. Leases for nonresidential (commercial) properties tend to be more complicated. Some of the terms covered in this chapter apply to leases in general. Other terms relate to specific issues, describing clauses that may be found in some leases but not others.

Leases are prepared by the landlord or the landlord's attorney. The landlord may use standard lease forms that are available online or they may prepare their own. Remember, a lease is a legal document. Some sound advice: Consult an attorney before signing a lease or any legal document.

The terms in this chapter will give you a good idea of different types of leases and how they work. Throughout these pages, you will also learn some of the more important terms and conditions in a lease and a few details of how leases are managed. You should walk away with a firmer understanding of how these legally binding agreements work.

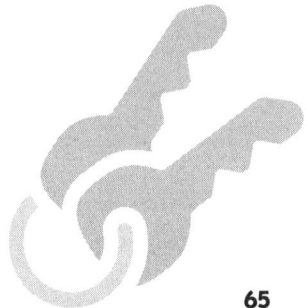

## assignment

**What it is:** a process where a new tenant agrees to take over the remaining term and conditions of a lease

**How it works:** When a tenant wants to get out of their lease, an assignment of the lease to a new tenant may be possible. An assignment theoretically removes the original tenant from any responsibility for the lease. Unlike the sublease (when a tenant leases to another tenant), the original tenant is removed from day-to-day responsibility of managing the assignment, such as collecting the rent and paying it to the landlord. However, if the assignee (person who takes the assignment) proves to be a bad tenant, the original tenant may be held responsible.

**How it is used:** The landlord agreed to the **assignment** of the remaining eight months of the lease.

## base rent

**What it is:** the monthly fee for renting a property/space that the tenant pays before any additional charges are added

**How it works:** Base rent is a term primarily used in leasing commercial space. Most commercial space is leased using some form of net lease. This means that in addition to the rent (base rent), there will be additional charges to be paid on behalf of the landlord, such as taxes and insurance costs. During the term of the lease, the base rent will not change except in accordance with an escalation clause that had been agreed to when the lease was signed. The additional charges may change from time to time.

**How it is used:** The **base rent** was $40.00 per square foot.

## base year

**What it is:** the first year of the lease and on which the expenses to be paid by the tenant are calculated

**How it works:** In leases where the tenants are expected to pay some or all of the building expenses, those expenses are calculated based on the first or base year of the lease. These calculations vary depending on the lease negotiations. For example, as an inducement to the tenant, the landlord waives the first year's building expense payment. The tenant agrees to pay their proportionate share of the building expenses beginning in the second year. An audit is then conducted of the base year to establish that amount. Subsequent years' calculations would be made based on that first year's expenses. The base year also means the date from which all rent increases will be calculated.

**How it is used:** The tenant agreed to pay their 10% proportionate share of the taxes and insurance above the **base year** amount.

## CAM (common area maintenance) fees

charges to tenants for upkeep of building areas used by everyone

**What it is:** costs to the tenants in commercial building leases to maintain areas used by all tenants and visitors

**How it works:** Commercial buildings have areas that are for the exclusive use of the tenant (referred to as the gross leasable area) and areas such as lobbies and hallways used by all tenants and visitors. In the net leases typically used in these buildings, the tenant agrees to pay for a share of the maintenance of these common areas. The tenants are either charged a flat fee or a proportionate share relative to the amount of space they rent.

**How it is used:** The tenant agreed to pay 20% of the **CAM fees** since they were renting 20% of the building space.

## early termination clause

a way to end the lease before the actual termination date

**What it is:** a statement in the lease that gives the conditions where a tenant can end the lease early or the reasons a landlord may end the lease early

**How it works:** On the tenant side, an early termination clause will have conditions such as a specific date that the lease can be terminated (for example, at the three-year anniversary of a five-year lease). In addition, the clause will most likely have a financial settlement amount to be paid to the landlord.

On the landlord side, conditions such as nonpayment of rent or violation of the use of the premises may result in early termination by the landlord.

**How it is used:** Both the landlord and the tenant wanted **early termination clauses** in the lease.

## fair market rents

rental rates established by the government

**What it is:** the federal government, through the US Department of Housing and Urban Development (HUD), establishes rental rates for federal housing programs

**How it works:** The federal government, through grants and subsidies, is involved in providing housing for lower- and middle-income tenants. These programs are subject to limitations on the rent that can be charged. The fair market rent is established for various locations to account for differences in the economy from one place to another in the United States, using studies of the rental market as well as income levels in various parts of the country.

**How it is used:** The town financial adviser checked the HUD **fair market rents** before proceeding with the housing project to see if it would meet the financial needs of the local citizens.

## GLA (gross leasable area)

amount of a property's space that can generate income

**What it is:** the space within a building that can be rented to one or more tenants

**How it works:** Gross leasable area (GLA), also called rentable space, is the total amount of building space that can generate income through rent. It is the space available for exclusive use by the tenants. It does not include common areas. The term may be used to identify the total gross leasable space in a building or the gross leasable space rented to a single tenant. Common areas, such as hallways, elevators, and lobbies, are included in a calculation known as gross floor area.

**How it is used:** The building contained 100,000 square feet of **GLA**.

## gross lease

**What it is:** when the tenant pays the landlord the rent, and the landlord pays all the building expenses

**How it works:** The name of this lease (*gross* meaning "total") comes from the fact that the rent to the landlord is gross, just like your gross salary. To get to the net lease income, the landlord must pay all the building expenses. This may include tasks like maintenance of common areas/driveways and work on the perimeter of the building. All of this work costs money, and it comes out of the gross rent payments. Even if the tenant is required to pay for things like their own utilities, the lease is still considered gross.

**How it is used:** Even though the tenants had a **gross lease**, the landlord made them pay for their own heat and parking.

## ground lease

a way to rent vacant land

**What it is:** a lease that only covers unoccupied land

**How it works:** Ground leases (also called land leases) technically can be any lease of a vacant piece of property, such as land for farming or a parking lot. The most common use of the term is for a long-term lease for property on which the tenant will construct a building for their use, to rent to others, or even for sale if the lease permits. The usual time frame for a ground lease can be anywhere from 50 to 99 years. The disposal of the building will be stated in the lease as to whether it will go to the property owner or be torn down.

**How it is used:** The company really liked the property, but because it wasn't for sale, they tried to get a **ground lease**.

## lease (lease agreement)

the written agreement between a property owner (landlord) and tenant

**What it is:** in most places, all real estate agreements must be in writing (this includes leases, with an exception in some places for leases under a year)

**How it works:** A lease contains basic information establishing the rights and duties of the landlord and the tenant. The lease will identify the parties involved, the space to be rented, the term (time frame) of the lease, the rent to be paid, and such other conditions that will affect the landlord and the tenant. A lease is considered a bilateral contract (two parties agree) that obligates both landlord and tenant; this document is legally binding on both sides.

**How it is used:** They couldn't wait to sign the **lease** for the new apartment.

## lease extension

*a continuation of the existing lease after the expiration date*

**What it is:** the ability to extend the length of time the existing lease remains in effect

**How it works:** A lease extension is a way to extend the terms of the lease without preparing a new lease or extensively changing the terms of the lease. This extension is a relatively simple way to continue the landlord-tenant relationship with the original terms of the lease intact. Minor modifications are possible, but unlike the lease renewal option, a new lease does not need to be written. The extension should be in writing.

**How it is used:** The tenant wanted to stay another year and asked the landlord for a **lease extension**.

## lease renewal option

*a way to continue a leasing arrangement*

**What it is:** a clause written in the original lease that states the terms for continuing the lease past its expiration date

**How it works:** A lease renewal option written into the original lease gives the tenant (lessee) the right to renew the lease provided they meet the terms in the option clause. The option clause could have various conditions, including a rent increase. The option is always in favor of the tenant. The landlord has no option since they can't force the tenant to stay beyond the lease expiration date. Lease renewal options are more common in commercial property leases.

**How it is used:** The tenant decided to exercise the **lease renewal option** and stay for another five years.

## lease term

the time frame of a lease

**What it is:** the span of time in which the lease will be in effect

**How it works:** The lease term is the total time from the beginning date to the end date of a lease. For example, a lease that begins on June 1, 2027, and ends on May 31, 2029, has a twenty-four-month or two-year lease term. Residential leases typically run for one or two years. Commercial leases tend to have longer terms of three to five years but may be longer or shorter. All lease terms are negotiable.

**How it is used:** The tenant decided to ask for a longer **lease term** of five years.

## leasehold/leased fee estate

the legal ownership interests of the tenant and landlord

**What it is:** descriptions of the technical, legal ownership interest of the tenant and landlord, respectively

**How it works:** These are primarily legal terms. The word *estate* is used to describe any legal interest in a piece of property. The tenant has the leasehold estate (they hold the lease), which allows them certain rights like exclusive use of the leased premises.

The leased fee estate is another term for an ownership interest in a property. The owner (or landlord) owns the fee of the property subject to the lease they have agreed to, which puts a limitation on their use. So, the owners are said to have a leased fee estate interest.

**How it is used:** The broker explained to the tenant that they would have a **leasehold estate** interest in the property while the landlord would have a **leased fee estate** interest.

## leasing commissions

fees paid to licensed real estate professionals for leasing services

**What it is:** landlords will often use real estate professionals—brokers and salespeople—to help find tenants; these professionals expect to be paid a fee

**How it works:** The two issues that must be resolved with respect to leasing commissions are who pays and how much. The determination of who pays is a matter of local custom and negotiation. In most cases, in both residential and commercial leases, the owner/landlord is responsible to pay the commission. However, this can vary, especially in high-demand areas. Residential commissions are usually paid in one payment. Because commercial leases are usually longer than residential leases, commissions sometimes are paid over the lifetime of the lease.

**How it is used:** The broker agreed to be paid their **leasing commission** over the first three years of the five-year lease.

## load factor

### the difference between usable and rentable square footage

**What it is:** a percentage number that accounts for the difference between what the tenant gets exclusive use of and what they pay for in a commercial building

**How it works:** The load factor for a building accounts for the difference between the space the tenant gets exclusive use of and the common areas like hallways and lobbies. Suppose there's a building with 100,000 square feet of total space and 90,000 square feet of usable (exclusive) space: 100,000 ÷ 90,000 = 1.11 load factor. Now, suppose a tenant needs 40,000 square feet of usable space. Multiply usable space by the load factor: 40,000 × 1.11 = 44,400 square feet of rentable space. The rent per square foot is multiplied by the rentable square foot number to get to the total rent.

**How it is used:** The tenant looked for the building with the lowest **load factor** so they would get the most usable square footage for their money.

## market rent

### what tenants are paying, and landlords are asking, for rent

**What it is:** an estimate of what the typical tenant is paying in rent for a particular kind of space

**How it works:** In any area, landlords and tenants are constantly negotiating and agreeing to rent amounts and terms. The market rent is based on gathering information about these transactions. To determine what to charge prospective tenants, a new owner of an apartment building might gather information on what several landlords are charging for two-bedroom apartments in the area. Assuming all these rentals are arm's length transactions (a deal between two strangers), this could be considered the market rent for this type of apartment. The more data that is collected, the more accurate the market rent estimate will be.

**How it is used:** The landlord studied the **market rent** in the area to see what they could charge for the vacant office space in their building.

## net lease

### a type of lease used for commercial rental

**What it is:** a rental arrangement where the tenant pays some of the building's expenses as part of their overall rental charge

**How it works:** The net lease, in contrast to the gross lease, requires the tenant to pay one or more (but not all) of the expenses paid by the landlord in a gross lease. For example, in a net lease, the tenant will most likely pay the property taxes. The amount and specific expenses that the tenant will pay are negotiable. In no case would the tenant pay all the building's expenses. The net lease is typically used for nonresidential, commercial spaces.

**How it is used:** The tenant agreed to a **net lease** that required that they pay a portion of the property taxes and insurance.

## percentage rent

### variable rent based on a percentage of income

**What it is:** a rent that is calculated based on a percentage of income of the tenant's business

**How it works:** Percentage rent is most often used in retail properties. A base rent is set that does not change from month to month. In addition to the base rent, the tenant is required to pay a percentage of their business income above a certain amount. For example, a tenant could be required to pay $1,000.00 per month plus 5% of gross sales above $100,000. Until the business income reaches $100,000, only the base rent will be due. A percentage lease can be either gross or net.

**How it is used:** The tenant was able to negotiate a lower base rent but had to agree to a higher **percentage rent**.

## proportionate share

### a way to fairly share a building's expenses

**What it is:** a division of building expenses according to the proportion of the building that each tenant rents

**How it works:** In any type of net or triple net lease, a tenant will be responsible for the building's expenses. These expenses do not include debt service (the mortgage loan payment). If there are multiple tenants in a building, the proportionate share method is a fair way to distribute the payment responsibilities. Proportionate share works by calculating the individual rental spaces as a proportion (percentage) of the total building space. For example, if Company XY rents 5,000 square feet of rentable space in a 50,000-square-foot building, they are renting 10% of the building (5,000 ÷ 50,000). If the tax bill for that year is $30,000, Company XY is responsible for 10%, or $3,000.

**How it is used:** The owner told the tenant that under the terms of their lease, the tenant would be responsible for a **proportionate share** of all the building's expenses.

## rent abatement

### a temporary reduction in rent

**What it is:** a reduction in rent for a period of time due to conditions that may or may not be spelled out in the lease

**How it works:** Although a rent abatement may be given by the landlord at any time for any reason, typically it is done when the premises become uninhabitable or severely limited in usability because of something like a fire or flood. For example, in a commercial lease situation, suppose part of the space was unusable due to water damage caused by a plumbing leak. The landlord might then agree to reduce the rent by 50% until the damage was repaired and the space was again usable. The possibility of a rent abatement may be written into the lease describing the circumstances under which an abatement could be granted.

**How it is used:** Due to the fire, the landlord granted the tenant a 100% **rent abatement** for the three months it would take to repair the space.

## rent concessions

### benefits provided to the tenant by the landlord

**What it is:** a landlord will sometimes offer an incentive to the tenant to make leasing space in the building more attractive

**How it works:** Rent concessions, as incentives to a prospective tenant or a tenant thinking about renewing a lease, can take many forms, such as a month or more of no (or reduced) rent. They could also come in the form of a lower initial deposit. The landlord may also offer free upgrades, say a high-end gas range in an apartment. Concessions may also be in the form of services. If the landlord charges the commercial tenant for office cleaning, a year's free cleaning could be offered. A residential building that has a membership fee gym could have the fee waived for a year.

**How it is used:** The landlord was prepared to offer three months of free rent and a new refrigerator as **rent concessions** to the tenant.

## rent control

### government control of rents

**What it is:** a government regulation that limits rent prices

**How it works:** Rent control is when state and local governments, on behalf of tenants, will sometimes pass laws that govern the maximum amount a landlord can charge for rents for an apartment as well as increases in rent. They may also limit deposit amounts. The term *rent control* itself is generic, meaning that one municipality may call it rent control while another may call it a tenant protection act or something similar. There may be state rent control programs that affect the entire state, as well as local programs that differ from one another. Rent control laws sometimes will only affect residential units above a certain number of apartments.

**How it is used:** The buyer had to consider the effect of the **rent control** laws when deciding on which investment property to buy.

## rent escalation clause

**What it is:** a provision in the lease to automatically increase the rent for the following year according to a formula, typically in leases longer than a year

**How it works:** Landlords always want to be protected from rising costs for operation of the property. For periods longer than a year, some level of protection can be built into the lease with a rent escalation clause. Escalation clauses are agreed to when the lease is signed. The escalation clause may be a straightforward agreement that on the anniversary date of the lease, the rent will increase by a certain percentage. In other cases, the increase might be based on some known index like the Consumer Price Index (CPI), which is generally considered to be a measure of inflation (rising prices) over time. The clause could also be a combination of the two. Rent escalation clauses can be used in both residential and commercial property leases.

**How it is used:** The tenant knew that according to the **rent escalation clause** of their lease, on the anniversary of the lease their rent would go up by at least 2% plus whatever the CPI increase was.

## rentable space

**What it is:** a term and measurement used in commercial buildings to calculate the base rent (the rent paid without extras) a tenant will pay

**How it works:** Commercial buildings typically have common spaces like hallways, elevators, and lobbies that are used by all the tenants and their visitors. The owners add a portion of this space (in square feet) into the usable area (space exclusively for the use of the tenant) leased by the tenant. The total common space is divided up proportionally to each tenant to arrive at rentable space. For example, suppose a tenant is renting 10% of the gross usable space in a building that has 10,000 square feet of common space. Ten percent of that space, 1,000 square feet, would be added to 5,000 square feet of usable space to come up with 6,000 square feet of rentable space. The total rent would be calculated on that number.

**How it is used:** The tenant signed a lease for 10,000 square feet of **rentable space** knowing their usable space would be about 15% less.

## sublease

### a tenant's lease to another tenant

**What it is:** an arrangement where a tenant rents their unit or space to someone else who is designated a subtenant

**How it works:** There are circumstances under which a tenant may want to leave their space before the end of the lease. They may also have circumstances such as an extended overseas work assignment that will take them away from their apartment. In such cases, usually with the landlord's approval, the tenant can create a lease with a third party to take over the space until the original lease expires or until the tenant returns. In a sublease, the original tenant remains responsible for the rent or damage done to the space. A sublease requires more hands-on management of the new tenant than an assignment does. The original tenant needs to be sure that the rent is collected from the subtenant and forwarded to the landlord on time. The tenant also needs to be sure that no damage is done to the space that they would be held responsible for.

**How it is used:** The tenant remained responsible for the rent on the **sublease** even though the landlord agreed to accept rent directly from the subtenant.

## termination on sale clause

### sale of the property can end a lease

**What it is:** a clause in a lease that allows the owner to terminate (end) the lease if the owner decides to sell the property

**How it works:** A property owner may wish to retain the right to deliver the property with no tenants if the new owner wants the property vacant. A termination on sale clause relieves the new owner of the normal responsibility of taking over previous leases. A buyer may wish to use the property for their own business or, in the case of residential property, to live in. The clause is not mandatory for the owner, who may leave the leases in place if that is the new owner's wish. The clause usually carries notice requirements that the owner must follow.

**How it is used:** The seller advised the buyer that they had a **termination on sale clause** in the lease so they could deliver the property vacant if that's what the buyer wanted.

## TIA (tenant improvement allowance)

an incentive the landlord gives to the tenant

**What it is:** in commercial real estate, this allowance is money or credits given to the tenant to help them customize their rented space for business needs

**How it works:** To make their building more attractive to tenants, landlords will sometimes provide a tenant improvement allowance (TIA) to help the tenant customize the space for their needs. The allowance may be in the form of credits on their rent or a cash outlay on the part of the landlord, which may or may not have to be paid back over the term of the lease. The TIA is also known as a tenant allowance (TA), build out, fit out, or leasehold improvement allowance.

**How it is used:** The landlord offered them a **TIA**, half of which had to be paid back in the first three years of the lease.

## triple net lease

a typical commercial property lease

**What it is:** this lease type requires the tenant to pay all the property's expenses in addition to their base rent

**How it works:** Unlike the net lease, which requires the tenant to pay some of the property expenses, the triple net lease requires the tenant to pay *all of* the property's expenses except debt service (the mortgage loan payments). Some examples of things they would have to pay would be real estate taxes, building insurance, and operational expenses like utilities and maintenance. The use of the term *net* three times to describe this lease is because the rent to the landlord is completely net since the tenant has paid all the expenses.

**How it is used:** Under the terms of the **triple net lease**, the tenant agreed to pay taxes, insurance, maintenance, and utilities for the property.

## usable space
area exclusively for the use of the tenant

**What it is:** a location in commercial buildings that is for the exclusive use of the tenant

**How it works:** In commercial buildings, there usually is common space such as hallways and lobbies that *all* tenants and visitors use. Additionally, there is space that is leased to tenants for only their use. This is called usable space. Usable space is considered to be the space enclosed by the walls and doors that is used exclusively by the tenant. In calculating rent, a portion of the common space is added to the usable space. This is called rentable space and is the space that the rent is calculated on.

**How it is used:** The **usable space** in the building was about 10% smaller than the rentable space.

# CHAPTER 6

# Tax Issues

A real estate investor needs to know quite a bit about taxes. The first thing they need to know is the name of a good accountant familiar with real estate investments. So, when talking to that accountant, understanding the terms associated with real estate investment tax issues will be extremely helpful.

Now, if the government just wanted to collect money, the tax code would be very simple. How much did you make? Send us some. However, the government also uses the tax code to discourage or encourage certain economic behaviors. Fortunately, one of the things that they try to encourage is real estate investment. There are provisions in the tax code specifically geared toward helping real estate investors. There are provisions that you might not be able to take advantage of as a homeowner, but they are of great benefit to you and your bottom line as an investment property owner.

The terms in this chapter will give you a thorough understanding of the issues you will deal with in paying your taxes, as well as the provisions that are designed to help you make money with your investment. There's a little bit of math in these definitions for clarity of what each term is all about, but don't be too concerned. That's what accountants are for.

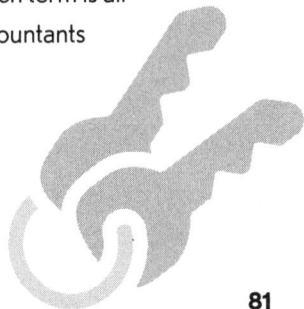

## assessed value

value used for taxes

**What it is:** the worth placed on a piece of property when calculating the taxes due on the property

**How it works:** The assessed value is a price placed by a local assessor that compares a property to others in the area. The assessed value can be almost any percentage of the true value of the property depending on state and local law. So, if a town assessed a property at 50% (the assessment ratio), the assessed value of a $300,000 house would be $150,000. Some states may have laws permitting different assessment ratios based on property type. Some municipalities may allow reductions in the assessed value for veterans, seniors, or other groups. The tax rate is multiplied by the assessed value to arrive at property taxes due.

**How it is used:** The owner was surprised at the **assessed value** of the property and thought about filing an appeal.

## capital gains tax

tax paid on the profit from a sale

**What it is:** a tax paid on the profit made when a property bought at one price is sold at a higher price (this profit is called a capital gain)

**How it works:** Unlike regular property taxes paid each year, capital gains taxes are paid once when something is sold at a higher price than it was bought for. Capital gains taxes apply to any asset (something valuable) like stock or land. The federal and most state governments collect these taxes. The long-term (owned over a year) capital gains tax rate is generally lower than the regular income tax rate. The short-term (under a year) rate is usually the regular income tax rate.

**How it is used:** The owner sold the property for a million dollars more than they paid for it, so they owed **capital gains tax** on the sale.

## capital gains tax exclusion

a special exception for homeowners

**What it is:** this allows qualified homeowners who sell their own home at a profit to then deduct a portion of their capital gain from being taxed

**How it works:** The federal government has provided some tax relief for homeowners who sell their primary residence at a profit, referred to as a capital gains tax exclusion. Certain conditions apply to this process and, if qualified, homeowners may deduct a portion of their capital gain before taxes are applied. The exemption applies only to a primary residence and not an investment property. Homeowners should consult with their accountant to determine if they qualify for the exemption.

**How it is used:** When they sold their house, they were able to qualify for the **capital gains tax exclusion** and ended up paying no capital gains tax.

## corporate tax structures

ways to minimize taxes

**What it is:** various ways to own property that may affect taxes

**How it works:** Corporate tax structures describe the several ways to own property from an organizational point of view that may also have an effect on taxes. For example, a person can own investment property through individual (sole) ownership or through a corporation. Two or more people owning property together will need a different ownership structure than an individual, like a partnership arrangement. A limited liability company (LLC) may provide some of the protections and advantages of a corporation without some of the drawbacks. These organizational structures have implications for liability, but they may also influence the amount of income tax paid on the property's income. Attorneys and accountants should be consulted to determine the best ownership structure in any given situation.

**How it is used:** The two owners consulted their accountants to determine the best **corporate tax structure** for their real estate investments.

## cost segregation

a way to reduce taxes

**What it is:** a tax strategy that can help reduce income taxes by maximizing depreciation deductions (e.g., allowing a deduction from building income of the cost of new air conditioning equipment separately and faster than the normal depreciation of the building)

**How it works:** The government allows different assets to be depreciated on different schedules (faster or slower). Cost segregation works by examining an investment property and separating out (segregating) different parts of the building into the various classes that the government allows. For example, equipment like the building's air conditioning system might depreciate more quickly than the building itself. Generally speaking, the more depreciation that can be taken, the lower the amount of taxes due. This can be especially useful in the early stages of building ownership.

**How it is used:** The owner brought in engineering and architectural experts to do a **cost segregation** study of the building.

## depreciation (economic)

a loss in value

**What it is:** from an economic perspective, when an asset loses value from one point in time to another

**How it works:** Depreciation, in the case of real estate, is when a property is worth a certain amount and, later on, the property is worth less. The term *depreciation*, when relating to the economy, describes a loss in value whether you own the property or not. Depreciation of a real estate asset can occur for many reasons. An overall downturn in the market, a rise in interest rates, or an economic change in the location, among other reasons, can cause a loss in value.

**How it is used:** The investor carefully watched the market for office buildings in the area to determine if the **depreciation** in value was continuing.

## depreciation (tax)

a theoretical loss in value reflected in tax calculations

**What it is:** in real estate, depreciation is based on the theory that buildings wear out over time; the government permits a tax deduction from income based on this theoretical loss in value

**How it works:** Depreciation, as a tax concept, allows an owner to deduct a certain amount of a building's value from the income of that building before income taxes are calculated. For example, suppose a building's annual income was $50,000 and the appropriate depreciation schedule allowed a $10,000 deduction. The taxable income would be $40,000. In other words, taxes would only be paid on $40,000. The government controls the depreciation schedule based on the building type (residential or commercial). The annual depreciation amount is related to the original purchase price of the property and the value of the building. The land is not depreciable. The term *cost recovery* is often used interchangeably with *depreciation*, though they're not exactly the same.

**How it is used:** The owners were able to deduct $15,000 each year from the property's income, using the allowed **depreciation**.

## depreciation recapture

### a form of taxable capital gains

**What it is:** capital gains profit due to tax depreciation (a theoretical loss in value reflected in tax calculations) calculated when a property is sold

**How it works:** Depreciation taken for tax purposes reduces the value of the property on paper. When the property is sold, assuming there is a profit on the sale, that profit is broken into two categories: the profit made by selling the property for more than the original purchase price, and the depreciated value of the property rather than the original purchase price as a base. The difference between the depreciated base and the original purchase price is considered depreciation recapture. Both are subject to taxes, but at different rates.

Suppose a property was bought for $500,000. The owner took $30,000 in depreciation over the ownership period. In effect the property's value was reduced by $30,000, which made the adjusted basis $470,000. Now, suppose the property was sold for $600,000. The owner would owe regular capital gains taxes on $100,000 profit and recapture taxes on $30,000. Long-term (1+ year) capital gains tax rates are usually different from recapture tax rates.

**How it is used:** The owner knew that they'd have to pay **depreciation recapture** taxes when they sold the property.

## estate tax

### tax due when a person dies

**What it is:** federal and state taxes that must be paid upon the death of the former estate owner

**How it works:** An estate (in its tax-related definition) is usually everything of value that a person owns. An estate tax becomes payable on the death of the estate owner based on the total value of the estate at the time of the death. Some states have no estate tax. Those with estate tax may have limits, where the tax is due only if the estate is worth more than a certain amount. The federal limit is relatively high and may change from time to time. An estate tax is also called an inheritance tax or a death tax.

**How it is used:** The family was glad that their parents had moved to a state with no **estate tax**.

## flip tax

### the tax that's not a tax

**What it is:** a fee paid when selling a condominium or cooperative

**How it works:** The term *flip tax* is misnamed because it is *not* a tax paid to the government. In some condominium and cooperative developments, a fee is charged upon sale of the unit. The fee is paid to the homeowners association or co-op board for maintenance of the complex or building. It may be calculated in various ways, such as a percentage of the sale price or flat fee.

**How it is used:** The sellers did not like the idea of having to pay the association a **flip tax** for selling their co-op.

## income tax

### annual tax paid based on income

**What it is:** tax paid as a percentage of a person's income, or generally what they earn on an ongoing basis

**How it works:** Income taxes are the primary source of funds to operate the federal government and most state governments. These taxes are based on annual income, like a paid job or an investment, minus tax deductions. A percentage tax rate is then applied to that amount (taxable income) to come up with taxes owed. An individual will have different tax deductions for personal income than they would from a real estate investment.

**How it is used:** The property owner's **income taxes** are due April 15 unless they get an exemption.

## passive income

### income with little work

**What it is:** an income type with money coming from sources that require little to no work

**How it works:** Passive and active income are defined by the Internal Revenue Service (IRS) and have to do with the amount of active participation a person has in earning the income. A salaried job generates active income. Passive income may include income from real estate investments that have little to no owner involvement in day-to-day management.

The federal government makes rules determining if income is active or passive. The issue with determining income type is how each is treated for tax purposes by the government. Depending on the current rules, different treatment of passive income's tax rates and allowable deductions may make it advantageous to actively manage the investment property. The owner may have to determine what the government's definition of active involvement is to turn passive income into active income.

**How it is used:** The owner was willing to get more involved in the property's management if the **passive income** taxes were too high.

## property tax appeal

### reducing your property taxes

**What it is:** an appeal to reduce the property taxes; usually available in several different ways

**How it works:** Strictly speaking, a person cannot appeal their property taxes to get a reduction. The appeal is for a reduction in the assessed value of the property, which has the ultimate effect of reducing the property's taxes. The procedures for appeal vary by state, and it is often referred to as filing a grievance. There's usually some kind of tax appeal board at the municipal level. Some places have adopted a streamlined small claims court process. After that, it may be necessary to file a suit in court. Depending on local and state law, investment property owners or owners of commercial buildings may have to go directly to court to file their tax assessment grievance.

**How it is used:** Being new to the town and state, the property owner intended to find out what the **property tax appeal** procedures were.

## property tax

### tax paid on the value of property

**What it is:** state and local governments generally collect taxes on property to operate government services

**How it works:** Local governments and districts rely the most on real estate taxes. These taxes are levied (imposed) on real estate according to the property's assessed value, and they are due based on a local schedule. Real estate is the source of most local revenue due to its predictable value and the inability to hide its value. Failure to pay taxes may result in foreclosure. Some local governments also collect taxes on personal property.

**How it is used:** The first half of the **property taxes** were due in April.

## real property tax rates

### tax rates for real estate

**What it is:** rates used to calculate taxes on a piece of real estate

**How it works:** Property taxes are local or county taxes due for real estate. To calculate these taxes, multiply the assessed value of the property by the tax rate. The tax rate is set by the taxing authority and may vary among different types of property. For example, residential property might be taxed at a different rate than commercial property. Homeowners, as opposed to investors, might receive some type of tax relief if they qualify. The typical tax rate is expressed in dollars of taxes per $1,000 of assessed value (mill rate).

**How it is used:** After the proposed budget was presented for the year, the town council met to determine the **real property tax rate** for that year.

## tax credit

### a direct reduction of income tax

**What it is:** an allowance of money that can be subtracted from the income taxes that are owed to the government

**How it works:** A tax credit is an allowance, usually for doing something, that can be subtracted from the total amount of taxes due. By comparison, a tax deduction is a subtraction from income that's being taxed. If the amounts are the same, a tax credit is usually worth more than a tax deduction. In the case of a real estate investment, suppose the government wanted to encourage owners to install more energy-efficient heating systems. They might allow a tax credit for a portion of the money spent on the system.

**How it is used:** The government was offering a **tax credit** for the installation of new energy-efficient windows in any building with six or more apartments.

## tax deduction

an amount subtracted from income and not taxed

**What it is:** an expense or other allowance that is deducted from income

**How it works:** The government understands that they would get no tax money from an unsuccessful investment property. The government also recognizes that there are expenses involved in operating a successful rental property. Most expenses connected with operating an investment property are therefore tax deductions. Mortgage loan interest is another tax deduction. Depreciation is another allowable deduction. The result of taking these deductions is a reduction in the income that will be subject to income taxes.

**How it is used:** The owner was able to claim a large enough number of **tax deductions** that they paid almost no taxes.

## tax deferred exchange

a way to avoid capital gains taxes

**What it is:** a rule allowing for the trading of properties rather than selling one property and buying another

**How it works:** A tax deferred exchange allows for putting off (deferring) capital gains taxes because there are no capital gains that are realized, meaning the seller has received no money. Properties are traded instead of bought and sold.

These exchanges are complicated transactions using a qualified third party and observing specific rules about when certain things must happen.

The transaction is not a direct trade, but rather properties going through the third party to prevent the exchange of cash, which would trigger capital gains taxes. Exchange agents specialize in this type of transaction. The tax deferred exchange is often referred to as a 1031 exchange, referring to the section of the law that governs these exchanges.

**How it is used:** The seller avoided capital gains taxes by using a **tax deferred exchange** instead of selling their property.

## tax incentive

### relief from taxes

**What it is:** a temporary break from taxes to encourage development

**How it works:** The state or a local government may offer to delay or forgive property taxes to encourage developers to invest in a certain area. Companies are sometimes offered tax incentives to locate plants that will offer employment opportunities.

Tax incentives can work in a variety of ways. A full or partial reduction is usually called a tax abatement. Incentives can range from complete tax abatement (no taxes) for several years to a tax abatement schedule with a gradually increasing percentage of taxes being paid over several years until full taxes are paid.

**How it is used:** The town offered them a **tax incentive** if they would build their new housing development in the town.

## tax lien

### a legal claim against a property for unpaid taxes

**What it is:** a claim against property that through the appropriate legal process allows the lienholder to claim the property

**How it works:** For local property tax liens, the local municipal government will place a lien on the property for nonpayment of taxes. This ensures that the government can claim the property and dispose of it to pay off the unpaid taxes. There are state and local rules that may vary from state to state that govern when a lien may be placed on the property, how and when foreclosure may happen, and how the property is to be disposed of. The state and federal governments also have the right to place a lien on property for unpaid income or other state or federal taxes.

**How it is used:** The owner was able to satisfy the **tax lien** on the property.

## tax shelter

### a way to reduce income taxes

**What it is:** an investment that will reduce current or future income taxes

**How it works:** A tax shelter is usually an investment that, because of IRS tax provisions, reduces current or future income taxes owed to the government. A real estate investment can be a tax shelter because of its depreciation benefits. Other real estate investment tax benefits include the ability to deduct operating expenses, mortgage loan interest, and real estate taxes. The 1031 real estate exchange described in this book provides for a deferral of capital gains, but there are other types of tax shelters. For example, certain retirement accounts can reduce current taxes by allowing tax deductible contributions. Government bonds are exempt from federal and some state income taxes.

**How it is used:** The **tax shelter** provided by the building's depreciation helped with their overall tax situation.

## transfer tax

### a fee paid when ownership changes

**What it is:** a charge that must be paid at closing to state and/or local governments

**How it works:** A transfer tax, money due to the government when closing on a property, may be imposed by the state as well as local governments. This tax's existence and amount vary throughout the United States based on state and town/city; in some places it is only charged on property transfers where the transaction is over a certain amount. The transfer tax is usually paid by the seller but can be negotiated for the buyer to pay.

**How it is used:** They sold the property for $999,900 since the **transfer tax** only affected property over a million dollars.

# CHAPTER 7

# Valuation

Valuation plays an important role in all aspects of real estate, including real estate investment. While investing, the investor wants to have an accurate idea of the value of the property they are about to buy, but when that investor goes to the bank to apply for their mortgage loan, value becomes even more important. The bank will want to know an accurate value of the property, as that's what the amount of the loan will be based on.

Later, after the property is bought, an investor may want to examine the real estate taxes. The assessed value of the property, based on the market value of the property, may be challenged. As the property hopefully increases in value and equity increases, the investor may want to refinance the property. Value again will play a crucial role in how much money can be taken out of the property. Should the investor want to dispose of the property, knowing the value will be crucial to maximizing profit. If the property is passed on to heirs as part of an estate, determining value is still important in paying estate taxes.

If you've skipped around in reading this book, you may have come across a few terms in this introduction, like *equity,* that are unfamiliar. You will find them defined in various chapters. The terms we're about to discuss will give you a complete picture of what value is and how the valuation process works. It will also reference some of these other terms as you begin to see the interlocking elements of real estate investment.

## adjustment value

### dollar value of a property feature

**What it is:** the result of analyzing property sales to determine the value of particular features of the property

**How it works:** To make value adjustments (accounting for various features in a property) in the sales comparison approach, the value of each adjustment must be determined. For example, if an adjustment must be made for a fourth bedroom, the dollar value of that bedroom must be determined. This is done by analyzing previous sales of similar properties to determine what someone would pay for the additional bedroom. The value of an adjustment is not a cost to construct value but rather what someone would pay for that feature in a sale.

**How it is used:** The appraiser determined that the **adjustment value** of the second bathroom was $10,000.

## appraisal

### an estimate of value

**What it is:** an estimate of an asset's worth based on research

**How it works:** The term *appraisal* is used to describe the process of estimating value as well as the report of the conclusions of that process. It is interesting to note in the definition that value is not "calculated," created, nor conclusively stated. An appraisal is the best work that can be done using both analysis and experience, using the available data to arrive at the type of value that has been requested (most often, market value). Appraisers use three techniques to value property: the sales comparison approach, cost approach, and income approach. Each has its strengths, but an appraiser will use all three in any appraisal assignment to arrive at the most accurate estimate of value.

**How it is used:** The bank ordered an **appraisal** of the property to determine if the requested mortgage loan should be approved.

## arm's length transaction

### a deal between two strangers

**What It is:** a negotiation between 2+ unrelated (personal or business) people

**How it works:** The concept of the arm's length transaction is crucial to establishing market value. It means that the parties to the transaction, in this case a real estate sale, have no personal or business relationship to each other. So, the amount accepted by the seller and paid by the buyer is not influenced by their relationship.

Real estate valuation and appraisal work by appraisers and brokers reflects the marketplace. When estimating value, real estate professionals look at known sales of property in the area. If those sales do not reflect market value, it may affect the next property being valued. If a sister sells a home well below market value to her brother, an appraiser valuing a similar house may arrive at an incorrect value estimate. So, they use multiple property transactions to avoid such issues and assume that most transactions are arm's length.

**How it is used:** The sale of the house down the street didn't really reflect its true value—it wasn't an **arm's length transaction** because the buyer and seller were sisters.

## assemblage

combining two or more properties

**What it is:** when one individual acquires two or more properties next to each other (adjacent) and combines them into one parcel of land

**How it works:** An investment opportunity may present itself when multiple pieces of land can be purchased and assembled into one larger piece of property. The larger piece will often be more attractive to large-scale developers. It may also qualify for certain types of zoning advantages that the smaller parcels would not qualify for. In addition, the assembled property may be more valuable than the value of the individual properties added together.

**How it is used:** The vacant land for sale next to the property they just inherited made **assemblage** a good possibility.

## capitalization rate

a rate of return on an investment

**What it is:** the mathematical relationship between the net operating income and the sale price of the property

**How it works:** The capitalization rate is one element in the income capitalization approach to determining value when appraising investment-type properties. The net operating income (NOI) is divided by the sale price of the property to find the capitalization rate. For example, if the net operating income is $200,000 and the value or sale price of the property is $2,000,000, the capitalization rate is 10% ($200,000 ÷ $2,000,000).

Capitalization rates are usually estimated by examining known real estate sales using this formula. Once a capitalization rate is known in an area, it can be used to calculate the estimated net operating income of a prospective investment.

**How it is used:** They were fortunate that they had data on several sales that they could use to calculate the **capitalization rate** for buildings in that area.

## CMA (comparative market analysis)

comparing similar properties to determine a sale price

**What it is:** an analytical process for determining an asking price or offering price for a property

**How it works:** The comparative market analysis (CMA) is usually done by a real estate agent; they analyze recent sales, current properties on the market, and properties on the market for an extended period to arrive at a price, known as the listing or asking price, for a property to be offered for sale. The CMA can also be done for a buyer to guide them in making an offer on a property. In some markets, the CMA is called a *competitive* market analysis.

**How it is used:** After completing the **CMA**, the broker recommended a higher asking price than the sellers thought the property was worth.

## comp (comparable)

a property similar to the subject property

**What it is:** a property that is very similar (or identical) to the property being appraised (the subject)

**How it works:** The sales comparison approach to value directly compares the subject property to properties that have already sold. These properties, known as comparables or comps, should be as similar as possible to the subject property to provide good information about the value of the subject. The ideal comp, though seldom found, is an identical property that sold in the last few months. Other appraisal methods will use comps to extract useful information—for example, deriving a gross rent multiplier (GRM).

**How it is used:** The market had been slow, so the appraiser was having a hard time finding good **comps**.

## cost approach
### finding the value of a unique property

**What it is:** an appraisal technique especially suited for unique properties that may not have many comparable sales

**How it works:** The cost approach to value is used by appraisers to estimate the value of unique properties like a house of worship. This approach focuses on the value of the land and building as separate pieces of the whole. The technique estimates a replacement or reproduction cost for the building; subtracts physical, functional, and economic obsolescence costs (depreciation); and adds in the land value to arrive at an estimate of the property value. It should be noted that an appraiser, if possible, will use all three approaches—sales, cost, and income—when appraising any property.

**How it is used:** The appraiser used a sales comparison approach when appraising the property, but they also used the **cost approach** to help confirm the value estimate.

## cost per square foot
### a way to calculate construction cost

**What it is:** a general method to express the expense of building something

**How it works:** A dollar cost per square foot is sometimes used to state a rough calculation of the cost to build something. It includes all the hard costs of the construction itself as well as the soft costs like architectural fees. The cost per square foot is highly dependent on the quality of the material as well as the variable costs of labor in different locations. So, in places with higher wages, the cost per square foot would likely be higher.

**How it is used:** They estimated that the **cost per square foot** to build the house would be $300.00.

## DCF (discounted cash flow)

a way to analyze future income

**What it is:** a method used by appraisers to estimate property value based on various factors including estimates of future income, expenses, and inflation rates

**How it works:** Because a property is owned for a period of time, during which it's expected to earn money plus be sold at a profit, one method of analyzing present value is to estimate the value of those future cash flows. The discounted cash flow (DCF) technique basically attempts to answer the question "What should I pay for this investment today based on an estimate of future income from the investment?"

**How it is used:** The prospective buyer and the appraiser agreed to use a 10-year time frame to do the **DCF** analysis as a middle ground between the typical 5- or 15-year periods.

## discount rate

an interest rate related to the inflation rate

**What it is:** the rate used to account for the diminishing value of money over time

**How it works:** The discount rate is used in the discounted cash flow (DCF) calculation to arrive at a net present value (the value today of all future benefits of owning the property). Future income must be discounted to account for future inflation. For example, what would $100,000 ten years from now be worth today? Since we can't see into the future, it can only be an estimate. That estimate depends on the discount rate that is used to account for the loss in value over time. It should be noted that the term *discount rate* is also used to describe the interest rate charged by the Federal Reserve for short-term loans to commercial banks.

**How it is used:** They decided to do the discounted cash flow analysis twice, using the current **discount rate** and a more conservative rate.

## economic obsolescence

### a decrease in a property's value due to outside forces

**What it is:** a decline (depreciation) in a property's value due to circumstances beyond the control of the property owner

**How it works:** Economic obsolescence (or external obsolescence) is a component of the cost approach to value. It refers to things outside the realm of the owner's control; so, it can occur for a variety of reasons such as a zoning change, increasing crime in the area, or the construction of a negative land use nearby. It has been referred to as external obsolescence because it is due to conditions beyond the boundaries of the property and therefore not subject to the owner's control.

**How it is used:** When appraising the house, the appraiser considered the gas station across the street from the house a source of **economic obsolescence**.

## functional obsolescence

### outdated design features

**What it is:** a description of design features in buildings that are outmoded or do not conform to current market tastes

**How it works:** Functional obsolescence is a component of the cost approach to value. It can result in a decline in a property's value due to physical features that have become outdated due to changing tastes. An example in older homes is the presence of a single bathroom off the kitchen when the home has several bedrooms, especially if they're second-floor bedrooms. This once may have been an acceptable design, but not today. A new house with poor design features can also suffer from functional obsolescence.

**How it is used:** The **functional obsolescence** of the house has reduced the sale price, making it easier to use the savings to modernize it.

## functional utility

### how well the building works

**What it is:** an analysis of how well the physical aspects of a building support its intended use

**How it works:** Functional utility is related to functional obsolescence. It is an analysis of how well a building physically supports the use for which it was intended, incorporating modern trends in design and efficiency. For example, a house where a person had to go through one bedroom to get to another (tandem bedrooms) would have poor functional utility by today's standards. Some functional utility issues can be easily corrected. Others might require reconstruction at a level that would not be economically sound. The term *functional utility* has nothing to do with utilities. However, inadequate electrical service, for example, would be seen as an aspect of poor functional utility.

**How it is used:** The house had poor **functional utility** due to its low ceilings and poor insulation.

## GIM (gross income multiplier)

a way to compare property values

**What it is:** the mathematical relationship between the sale price and the gross annual income of a property

**How it works:** The gross income multiplier (GIM) is like the gross rent multiplier except that the GIM includes all property income—rental income or income from sources like parking or washing machines. The calculations and application are the same as the gross rent multiplier except that the gross rent multiplier only uses rental income. The GIM equals sale price divided by total gross annual income. The GIM is then multiplied by the total gross annual income of the prospective building to arrive at a suggested sale price. Multiple properties that have recently sold should be analyzed. The method should be used in addition to other approaches to value.

**How it is used:** Using the **GIM**, the investor identified two possible investments.

## GRM (gross rent multiplier)

a way to compare property values

**What it is:** the mathematical relationship between a property's sale price and its gross annual rental income

**How it works:** To use the gross rent multiplier (GRM), divide the sale prices of several recently sold properties by their total annual gross rental incomes. Assuming the several gross rent multipliers are not the same, one may be selected by taking an average or median (middle one) or choosing the one that is from the property most similar to the one under consideration. Then multiply the resulting GRM by the gross annual rental income of the prospective investment property. Using a one-property example: Suppose a 10-unit residential building has sold for $3,000,000. The gross annual rental income is $200,000. So, $3,000,000 ÷ $200,000 = a GRM of 15. Now suppose an investor is looking at a similar building for sale with a gross annual rental income of $150,000. By multiplying the GRM by the annual rental income of $150,000, the investor should pay $2,250,000 for the property.

**How it is used:** The investor first sorted out some possible property investments by using the **GRM**, then they called in an appraiser.

## income approach

estimating the value of commercial properties

**What it is:** an appraisal technique using the income of a property to estimate its value

**How it works:** The concept of capitalization is that the income and value of an income-producing property are related. The higher the income from the property, the higher the value. The income approach (or the income capitalization approach) analyzes income and expenses to arrive at the net operating income (NOI). The NOI is the annual income of the building minus all expenses except for the mortgage loan payments (debt service). The NOI is then divided by the capitalization rate to arrive at an estimate of value. The capitalization rate is derived by analyzing recent sales of similar properties and dividing the NOI (obtained by research through real estate agents and appraisers) by the sale price. The income approach is well suited to appraising investment properties because people buy investment properties to make money, so value and income are related.

**How it is used:** The **income approach** seemed to be the best technique to appraise the 50,000-square-foot office building.

## investment value

### value to a particular investor

**What it is:** a property's worth to an investor with a specific plan for the land

**How it works:** Investment value is the price a particular investor will pay for the property to accomplish a certain plan or goal. The investment value may be above the property's market value (what the general market would pay for the property). An investor might calculate that they can afford to pay $500,000 more than market value because their plan for the property will profit more than what the normal development of the property would generate. (They will make a large excess of $500,000.)

**How it is used:** The **investment value** of the property could be justified if they could get the necessary approvals to build the shopping center.

## land value

### the value of the land with or without a building on it

**What it is:** various valuation situations and techniques require someone to know the value of land whether vacant or improved, that is, with a building or other improvements on it

**How it works:** The value of a piece of vacant land will be a key component in deciding what the land can be developed for and the price that can be generated by the improved property. The cost approach to determining value requires a separate value estimate of the land when appraising the property. Economic depreciation cannot be applied to land, so the value must be separated out when calculating depreciation in the cost approach.

**How it is used:** A developer assessed that due to average sale prices of $300,000 and construction costs of $220,000, that the **land value** of each lot in a development was around $80,000.

## liquidation value

### value in a quick sale

**What it is:** the estimated value of property left on the market for less than a reasonable period of time

**How it works:** There are circumstances where properties must be sold in incredibly quick time frames. Foreclosures (when someone with a mortgage cannot afford to pay it), forced sales due to business or personal reasons, or anything that would have the property on the market for a shorter than normal period of time would likely result in a lower than market value price. Liquidation value is the estimated price that would result from such circumstances.

**How it is used:** The sale price ended up being slightly higher than the estimated **liquidation value**.

## market value
### a value without limitations

**What it is:** a specifically defined type of value that is the foundation of most real estate transactions and processes

**How it works:** Market value (or fair market value) has a very specific definition of being the most probable price a property will sell for in an open and fair market where both parties are acting freely without undue influence, both well informed and acting in their own best interest, and where the property is on the market for a reasonably sufficient length of time.

The transaction is assumed to be arm's length (with no relationship between buyer and seller). If you're the only one who knows about a property and you buy it, that sale price may not reflect market value. Or, if you buy a piece of property from your sister, that price may not reflect market value.

**How it is used:** The appraiser was able to use the property for their analysis of other properties because they knew the sale had met all the conditions for a **market value** transaction.

## NOI (net operating income)
### annual property income after expenses

**What it is:** the annual income from an investment property that remains after all building expenses are paid except the mortgage loan payment (debt service)

**How it works:** Net operating income (NOI) is one element in the income approach to determining value, which is used by appraisers to estimate the value of an investment-type property. The income approach calculates the net operating income, which is the total annual property income minus all expenses except for the mortgage loan payments (debt service). It then divides the NOI by the capitalization rate, which is derived from known recent sales of similar properties by dividing the NOI of the property by its sale price. The result of dividing the NOI by the capitalization rate is the estimated value of the property under consideration.

**How it is used:** The investor hoped that by investing in heating and better windows, they could lower energy costs and raise the **NOI** for the property.

## physical obsolescence

wear and tear on the property

**What it is:** the decline (depreciation) in the value of a building due to the aging effects of time

**How it works:** Physical deterioration of a building is inevitable because various components like the roof, siding, and mechanical equipment wear out with time and use. Preventive and corrective maintenance can keep some of this from occurring. Timely replacement of various components can also reduce the amount of physical obsolescence. Physical obsolescence is a component of the cost approach to determining property values.

**How it is used:** It was clear to the appraiser that the owner's maintenance program had significantly reduced the amount of **physical obsolescence**.

## plottage

the value advantage of several properties together

**What it is:** the additional value that might be created by the assemblage of multiple smaller parcels into one large parcel of property.

**How it works:** Larger properties may have particular advantages in the marketplace for development and certain zoning advantages. Assemblage (putting the parcels of property together) may generate those economic advantages. The difference between the assembled property value and the value of the individual properties added together is called the plottage, plottage value, or plottage increment. For example, suppose an investor bought three adjacent one-acre properties for $100,000 each and then was able to sell the new three-acre parcel for $500,000. The $200,000 profit would be the plottage value.

**How it is used:** The developer anticipated that by combining the four adjacent properties, they could be sold with an added **plottage** value of $300,000 to what was originally paid.

## price per square foot

a way to compare sale prices

**What it is:** a mathematical calculation that quickly compares sale prices of properties while still taking several factors into account

**How it works:** Price per square foot is the calculation of sale price (or asking price) divided by the total number of square feet of the structure. Suppose the asking price of a house is $400,000 and the size of the house is 2,000 square feet: $400,000 ÷ 2,000 square feet = $200 per square foot. This calculation automatically considers things like location, condition of the house, and other factors. If a buyer makes this calculation for several similarly sized properties, using either asking price or previous sale price, they can get an idea of what properties are selling for in a particular area.

**How it is used:** In the last six months, houses have sold for a **price per square foot** of between $200 and $300.

## real estate market cycle

the pattern of real estate supply and demand

**What it is:** a repetitive flow within the real estate market of high and low supply and demand

**How it works:** There are four phases to the real estate market cycle. Phase one is *recovery*, in which there is no new construction and vacancies are declining as existing properties are being rented. Phase two is *expansion*, where there is new construction and vacancies continue to decline. Phase three is *hyper supply*, as new construction continues and vacancies begin to rise. Phase four is *recession*, as construction projects are completed and vacancy rates continue to increase.

**How it is used:** The investor was being cautious about starting a new project because they thought they might be in the hyper supply phase of the **real estate market cycle**.

## reconciliation of value

### making the final value estimate

**What it is:** the process of analyzing all appraisal approaches and arriving at a single value estimate

**How it works:** Appraisers use as many approaches as possible to estimate the value of a property. These can include cost, sales, and income approaches to determine the value of commercial properties, and using the gross rent multiplier or gross income multiplier (two ways to compare property values using rent or income). The appraiser then analyzes the results from the various techniques. Techniques particularly suited to the property are prioritized, for example, the income approach to a commercial property. The data will also be examined to determine the reliability of different data. Finally, a single estimate of value will be presented: the reconciliation of value (which is also called value reconciliation or reconciliation).

**How it is used:** The appraiser did the **reconciliation of value** and was ready to write the appraisal report.

## replacement cost

### a modern equivalent of the price of a specific building

**What it is:** the cost to construct a modern replacement of the subject building (the property being appraised) using modern materials and standards

**How it works:** In the cost approach (one of the three approaches to value), appraisers must first estimate the cost of duplicating the building being appraised. However, the replacement cost is an estimate to replace the structure using modern materials, design, and standards as opposed to a reproduction cost, which is the cost to produce an exact replica of the structure. The replacement cost estimate will be for a new structure. This is important because the existing structure, which is being appraised, unless it is new, will have wear and tear due to usage and age. This will be considered as part of the cost approach process.

**How it is used:** The building had no historic or architectural significance, so the appraiser used a **replacement cost** estimate when appraising the property.

## reproduction cost

### cost to build a duplicate

**What it is:** in the cost approach to valuation, the price to construct an exact duplicate of a building

**How it works:** One of the methods used to appraise a property with a building on it uses calculations to determine what the structure is worth separate from the land; this is called the cost approach. If the building is of historic or architectural significance, a reproduction cost calculation may be used to find the cost to create an exact duplicate of the structure. Say a 200-year-old church had been designed by a noted architect. In appraising the building's value, a replacement cost (cost to replace using modern design standards and materials) wouldn't account for the value of the historic nature of the construction and materials.

**How it is used:** The appraiser decided to use a **reproduction cost** for the building since it was on the town's historic register.

## sales comparison approach

### a way to estimate residential property value

**What it is:** an approach using an analysis of comparable sales to estimate the value of residential property

**How it works:** The sales comparison approach, sometimes called the market approach, is an appraisal technique used primarily to appraise one- and two-family (unit) residential properties. The technique uses a detailed analysis of comparable properties that have recently sold. The properties' sale prices are adjusted for features that differ from the subject property (the property being appraised). The technique is based on the principle of substitution. If several similar properties sell within a certain price range, a similar property will likely be worth a price within that range.

**How it is used:** The appraiser used the **sales comparison approach** when appraising the house for the mortgage loan.

## sale price

the price something sells for

**What it is:** the actual amount, in dollars, that a piece of property has sold for

**How it works:** Sale price may seem to be an obvious term without much importance beyond telling us what something sold for, but in real estate, it can be very important in determining the value of other properties. Real estate values are not determined in isolation from one another. The values of properties in neighborhoods, communities, and school districts, even blocks, relate to one another. The comparative market analysis (CMA) is all about analyzing prices of similar properties that have recently sold to predict the price that another property should sell for.

**How it is used:** The broker looked at the **sale price** of several neighborhood properties to advise the seller what the asking price of their property should be.

## time adjustment

accounting for change in value over time

**What it is:** a number tweak that accounts for an increase or decrease in a property's value during the passage of time

**How it works:** In the sales comparison approach to determining property value, comparisons are made between the subject property (property being appraised) and comparables (properties similar to the subject property). Suppose one of the comparables sold almost a year ago, and during this past year, the real estate market for this property type went up 10%. To be truly comparable with the subject property now, that sale price would have to be increased by 10%. That 10% increase for what has happened this past year is called a time adjustment. Time itself is not the factor but rather market conditions that have changed over time. The adjustment can therefore be up, down, or flat.

**How it is used:** The investor analyzed the market for the past year and realized that a **time adjustment** for the comparable sale they found would decrease it 5% in value to reflect market conditions.

## value

### what something is worth

**What it is:** a concept that if someone wants something someone else owns, they offer goods, services, or money in exchange for the thing, ultimately agreeing to a value (price) for the exchange

**How it works:** There are different kinds of value. When the word *value* is discussed without any specifics, what is usually meant is value in exchange. What is something worth in exchange for something else, usually money? The primary aspect of value in exchange is that there is a market for the item, that is, someone who wants to sell and someone who wants to buy. That interaction is what creates value and affects how much value something has.

**How it is used:** No one would want to buy the old shack I grew up in, so it has little **value** to anyone but me; however, the land would be great for a housing subdivision, so the **value** is in the land.

## value adjustment

### accounting for various features

**What it is:** part of the sales comparison approach to valuation that gives a dollar value to various property features

**How it works:** The process of the sales comparison approach is to compare known sales to the subject property (property being appraised). Since properties are not identical, adjustments have to be made between the comparable (a property similar to the subject property) and the subject. For example, suppose the comparable sold for $300,000 and had three bedrooms, and the subject is identical but has four bedrooms. A value adjustment in dollars is made to answer the question of what the comparable would have sold for if it had four bedrooms.

**How it is used:** The appraiser added a **value adjustment** for a second bathroom to the comparable since the subject had two bathrooms and the comparable had only one.

## value in use

property value to a specific user

**What it is:** the value of a property to a specific user for a specific use

**How it works:** Most properties are appraised at market value, which is the value generated in the open real estate market. Sometimes a particular user might be able to take advantage of the property in a way another user may not, such as with a doctor's office in a house. On the other hand, the cost to modify that space for a non-doctor buyer may impair the value of a property compared to market value. Value in use reflects how useful the property would be to the specific owner rather than the general market. Or take a residential property with a multicar garage, lifts, special lighting, and other equipment suitable for automobile repair. Provided local zoning permits this as a home occupation, this property would likely have a significantly higher value for an auto mechanic, not to a regular buyer.

**How it is used:** Since the property provided an opportunity to have a professional office at home, the owners decided to have the house appraised for **value in use** and its regular market value to see if there would be any advantage in pricing.

# CHAPTER 8

# Buying and Selling

Throughout this book, you've learned terms important to finding property, financing property, and valuing property. This chapter will explain many of the terms associated with buying and selling property. At first glance, buying and selling property should be straightforward, especially when using a real estate agent.

On the contrary, using an agent presents issues that you, the buyer or seller, landlord or tenant, should be aware of. Real estate agents provide valuable services that can be of great help, especially as an investor. But it's important to understand who they represent in a transaction, how they get paid, and what services they can provide. The buying and selling process itself can be complicated only because it's something people don't do very often. So, there are many terms you've never heard or heard once, and you may not be very clear as to what these terms mean.

This chapter on buying and selling will give you a detailed look at the terms you may encounter with explanations that should help you better understand the buying and selling process. Real estate laws differ from one state to another, but this chapter will give you a good foundation from which you'll understand buying and selling and how to ask the right questions.

## agent

**What it is:** a person who represents a client in any kind of a transaction

**How it works:** In real estate transactions, brokers and their salespeople normally act as agents for the parties involved in the transaction. The term *agency* can refer to an organization like a real estate agency. However, agency can also mean the existence of some type of representative relationship between an agent and the person being represented. In real estate transactions, the broker is considered to be the agent, while the salespeople are subagents of the broker. The typical real estate agent acts as a special agent, which means they have the responsibility of working on a single transaction for the client. A general agent has broader responsibilities, such as a property manager to a client. A universal agent, rare in real estate transactions, handles all of a client's business matters.

**How it is used:** They hired XYZ Brokers to be their **agent** for the sale of their property.

## associate broker

a broker who works as a salesperson

**What it is:** a licensed broker who works under the supervision of another licensed broker

**How it works:** An associate broker is someone who has fulfilled all the requirements for the broker's license, but they choose to work under the license and supervision of another broker (the person acting between a buyer and seller or tenant and landlord). Achieving the broker's license can be seen as advancing in a real estate career since it requires a higher level of training and experience beyond that of a salesperson. However, establishing a real estate brokerage may not be everyone's ambition. The associate broker arrangement allows a salesperson to achieve the status of broker without opening a business.

**How it is used:** The **associate broker** did well in the negotiations on my behalf, and I would recommend them highly.

## bilateral contract

**an agreement that obligates both groups**

**What it is:** an agreement between two parties that requires each of them to fulfill their part of the agreement

**How it works:** The sales agreement to buy and sell a property is a typical example of a bilateral contract. In this type of agreement, the buyer is required to pay the funds required and go through with the purchase. The seller is also obligated to proceed with the sale. Either party may be forced to fulfill their promised obligations. A lease is another example of a bilateral contract in real estate.

**How it is used:** Since the sales agreement was a **bilateral contract**, once they signed it, they could be forced to complete the sale.

## broker

**the person acting between a buyer and seller or tenant and landlord**

**What it is:** any person in a transaction acting either as an intermediary (person in the middle) or representing one party or another

**How it works:** In real estate, a broker is an individual licensed by the state to perform certain activities on behalf of another person for a fee. Licensing requirements vary by state, but most states have a list of activities that only a licensed broker may perform. The "for another, for a fee" is important in this definition. An unlicensed person may always perform any activity they wish for themselves. An unlicensed person can usually help a friend or relative with real estate matters provided no fee is charged. State laws may vary, but, in general, to open and operate a real estate office, a person must be a licensed broker in that state.

**How it is used:** The couple hired a **broker** to help them find their first investment property.

## broker commission

**fee based on the sale price**

**What it is:** when the broker's fee is based on the final sale price

**How it works:** The commission model of paying for real estate services is the most typical fee arrangement. Basically, the higher the sale price of the property, the higher the fee to the broker (the person acting between a buyer and seller or tenant and landlord), thereby creating an incentive to achieve the highest price for the seller. It was also based on an old model of representation where only the seller was represented. The commission was frequently split between two brokers: one broker having offered the property for sale and another broker bringing a buyer to the transaction. The commission was further split with the salesperson in the brokerage who worked on the transaction. As buyer agency (a broker representing a buyer) became common, representation changed, but commissions were often still handled the same way.

**How it is used:** The seller thought **broker commissions** were set by the state but found out they were completely negotiable with each broker.

## buyer agency

### a broker representing a buyer

**What it is:** an arrangement where a broker agrees to represent the buyer just as a broker would represent a seller

**How it works:** For many years, brokers only represented sellers. Some years ago, buyer agency began to develop as buyers understood that they might need professional help to represent their interests too. The broker fee is still somewhat complicated with buyers either paying the buyer's agent fee directly, or the fee being paid through the seller's agent. Regardless, both sellers and buyers should expect their agents to provide a clear explanation of how seller's and buyer's agent fees will be paid.

**How it is used:** The buyer liked the idea of being represented in the transaction and looked for a brokerage that specialized in **buyer agency**.

## client

### the person the agent represents

**What it is:** in a real estate transaction, a person being represented by a real estate agent

**How it works:** In most real estate transactions, there are four people involved: the buyer and their agent (someone who represents someone else in a transaction), and the seller and their agent. Just as there are two agents, there are two clients: The buyer is the client of the buyer's agent, and the seller is the client of the seller's agent. Each agent owes their fiduciary duty (a legal/ethical relationship of trust) to their own client.

**How it is used:** The broker explained their duties to the new **client**.

## closing

### transferring ownership of the property

**What it is:** the term used to describe the actual transfer of ownership (the title) of a property

**How it works:** Closing occurs on a certain date where the ownership (or property title) goes from the seller to the buyer. The buyer owns the property on the day of closing when all documents are completed. The closing usually involves signing several documents and giving funds to the seller and other participants, like the title company. If financing has been used, there is also a mortgage closing at the same time. Closing costs are apportioned at this time. Closing can be done in person, by mail, or in escrow. Property ownership can be transferred by gift or means other than a sale, and the correct terms are *grantor* for the owner transferring the property and *grantee* for the person receiving the property.

**How it is used:** The **closing** was postponed due to a problem with the mortgage loan approval.

## closing in escrow

### a way to transfer property ownership

**What it is:** a way to complete the transfer of property ownership without being physically present

**How it works:** Closing in escrow (also called closing escrow) uses an escrow agent to handle all the documents necessary to transfer property ownership from one person to another. All necessary paperwork, including mortgage loan documents and funds, is sent to the agent. When all the necessary documents are in the agent's possession, the agent distributes them to the appropriate parties. In some areas, closing in escrow is common practice. It may also be convenient because of distance where an out-of-state purchaser may be involved.

**How it is used:** They decided to **close in escrow** since the buyer would be overseas for several months.

## contingencies

things that may stop a deal

**What it is:** issues that must be resolved before an agreement can be fulfilled

**How it works:** Contingencies are often found in sales agreements. They are mostly raised by the buyer and must be resolved before going ahead with the sale of the property. For example, the buyer will want assurance that they have obtained sufficient financing to proceed with the purchase, or maybe they ask that the property passes an inspection before proceeding. Someone buying vacant land may want to drill a well to prove there is water available and obtain septic system approval. Initially, a contingency is a requirement that must be fulfilled for the sale to proceed. However, contingencies can be negotiated after the contract is signed. For example, the cost of unacceptable items found in the inspection may be negotiated so that the sale may proceed.

**How it is used:** The market was so hot that the seller would not agree to let the buyer put any **contingencies** in the sales contract.

## contingency clause

contract clause that creates a condition

**What it is:** a statement in a contract that creates a condition for the contract to go forward

**How it works:** A contingency clause may be placed in a real estate sales contract (purchase agreement) to permit any reasonable condition to be met to move the contract forward or stop it. A typical contingency clause in a real estate sale contract is for the buyer to obtain approved financing for the purchase. Another clause is for the property to pass an inspection. A contingency clause that cannot be met will usually stop the contract from proceeding. However, contingency clauses are generally written so that if the contingency is met, the parties must proceed with the terms of the contract.

**How it is used:** The buyers put a **contingency clause** in the contract that the house had to pass a radon inspection.

## customer

### the third party in a transaction

**What it is:** the person or group being represented by another agent

**How it works:** If there are a buyer and seller who are each represented by a real estate agent (someone who represents someone else in a transaction), the following is the designation of the parties. The buyer client (the person the agent represents) is represented by a buyer's agent. The seller client is represented by a seller's agent. To the seller's agent, the buyer is a customer. To the buyer's agent, the seller is a customer. The customer is sometimes called the third party in this situation. The agents owe their fiduciary duty (a legal/ethical relationship of trust) and honesty to their clients.

**How it is used:** The broker explained to the buyer that they would consider them their client and any seller, a **customer.**

## deed

### the document showing property ownership

**What it is:** a legal document that shows the current and previous ownership of a property

**How it works:** A deed is used to transfer property ownership from one person to another. It has very strict requirements for it to be valid. For example, it must have what is called a legal description of the property. It must name the grantee (person receiving ownership) and be signed by the grantor (person giving ownership). The deed is normally prepared by an attorney and is the document that is recorded in the public records.

**How it is used:** The title insurance company took responsibility for recording the **deed** at the county clerk's office.

## designated agency

a way for a single brokerage to represent both the buyer and a seller

**What it is:** when two different salespeople under the same broker represent two different clients in the same transaction

**How it works:** In a situation where one broker and one salesperson are going to represent the two parties to a transaction, it may be possible to keep both interests somewhat separate by using designated agency. In this arrangement, the broker (the person acting between a buyer and seller or tenant and landlord) assigns one agent (salesperson or associate broker) to one side and another agent to the other side. Each agent agrees to maintain confidentiality from the other. Technically, it is still a form of dual agency (two people represented by the same agent) since the broker is the actual agent, but ideally it does protect the interests of each party. Both parties must agree to give informed consent (consent with complete understanding of the arrangement).

**How it is used:** The buyer and seller agreed to the **designated agent** arrangement rather than going to another broker.

## dual agency

two people represented by the same agent

**What it is:** a situation where two opposing parties to a transaction are represented by the same broker

**How it works:** Dual agency often occurs in real estate transactions because a broker/salesperson (the person acting between a buyer and seller or tenant and landlord) already has agreed to represent a seller, and later a buyer is interested in the same property. There are usually rules that govern dual agency. Typically, both parties must be informed of what dual agency is and must agree to it (informed consent). Because it is impossible to give complete fiduciary duty (complete and undivided loyalty) to two parties in the same transaction, dual agency is sometimes referred to as limited agency. Any fees that are normally paid to two different brokers in a single agency arrangement might be paid to one broker depending on the negotiations before or during the transaction.

**How it is used:** Since both parties agreed to the **dual agency**, they asked for a fee reduction.

## earnest money

### initial payment to secure the property

**What it is:** used to show that a person's interest in purchasing the property is sincere

**How it works:** Earnest money (or good faith money), ranging from 1% to 10% of the offering price, often accompanies the offer to purchase. The amount and use of earnest money may vary by local convention, state, or region within a state. It may also vary by the type of property: residential versus commercial. In some markets, after negotiations are conducted verbally, the purchase agreement (contract) is drawn up immediately. The agreement will usually call for at least a 10% deposit of the price. Depending on the terms of the written offer to purchase and/or the purchase agreement, the earnest money or deposit may be forfeited to the seller if the buyer decides not to go through with the transaction.

**How it is used:** The buyers decided to submit their offer in writing with a 1% **earnest money** amount.

## exclusive agency

### listing agreement where the owner may not have to pay

**What it is:** an agreement that allows the owner to avoid the broker's fee by selling the property themselves

**How it works:** In the exclusive agency listing agreement, the owner agrees to pay the broker (the person acting between a buyer and seller or tenant and landlord) a fee if the broker sells the property, but *only* if they sell the property. Unlike an exclusive right to sell agreement, under exclusive agency the owner retains the right to sell the property themselves without paying a fee. This works out in the owner's favor if they are able to find someone interested in buying without the help of the broker.

**How it is used:** The owner thought they might be able to sell the property themselves, so they were only willing to sign an **exclusive agency** listing agreement with the broker.

## exclusive agency buyer agency

### the broker may not get paid

**What it is:** an arrangement where the broker gets paid only if they achieve results

**How it works:** The exclusive agency buyer agency agreement is the buyer side of the seller's exclusive agency agreement. The buyer agrees to pay the broker (buyer's agent) if they are successful in finding a property to buy. If the buyer or another agent finds the property, the buyer does not owe a fee to the original buyer's agent. They likely would have to pay a fee to any agent who finds them a property.

**How it is used:** Since the buyer had many contacts who knew about the kind of property they wanted to invest in, they were only willing to sign an **exclusive agency buyer agency** agreement with the broker.

## exclusive buyer agency

### the broker will always be paid

**What it is:** an arrangement where a broker (agent) will always be paid

**How it works:** Exclusive buyer agency is the agreement where a broker will represent the buyer and will be paid their fee regardless of who finds the property for the buyer. The broker will be paid even if another agent or the buyer themselves finds the property. This is obviously a great setup for the agency, as they make money regardless of who does the final work for the buyer.

**How it is used:** The buyer already had several leads for the kind of property they needed so they didn't want to sign an **exclusive buyer agency** agreement.

## exclusive right to sell

### a listing agreement with a real estate agent

**What it is:** an agreement that gives a real estate broker, and only the broker, the right to sell your property

**How it works:** An arrangement for the exclusive right to sell, often just called an exclusive, is a listing agreement that an owner makes with a real estate broker (the person acting on behalf of the seller) to allow that broker to sell the property. Regardless of who might actually sell the property, including the property owner, that broker is owed a fee. It is the most typical real estate listing arrangement, and it's easier for the broker to make money in this arrangement than with the exclusive agency agreement, which allows the owner themselves to sell the property and not pay the broker a fee.

**How it is used:** The broker wanted to get an exclusive on the property and had to explain to the owner how an **exclusive right to sell** listing agreement worked.

## fee for service

### a different way to pay for real estate services

**What it is:** a relatively recent innovation that does not charge for real estate services as a percentage of the sale price of the property (commission)

**How it works:** In the fee for service arrangement, the client would pay for only those real estate services that they need. Payment would be made for the individual services whether the property was ultimately bought or sold. The advantage could be a lower overall price for the buyer or seller. There are brokers who offer this payment model in addition to the standard commission model. Fee for services may also be known as real estate consulting, menu of services, and a la carte services.

**How it is used:** They decided to look for a **fee for service** broker since they already knew quite a lot about real estate transactions.

## fiduciary duty

### loyal representation of someone

**What it is:** obligations that someone acting as a fiduciary has to the person they are representing

**How it works:** In real estate, the agent owes the client their fiduciary duty. This is a list of specific duties that they must adhere to in their work on behalf of the client. They may vary by state, but these are the essential duties included when discussing fiduciary duty: accounting, care, confidentiality, disclosure, loyalty, and obedience. Fiduciary duty includes the fact that the representative must put their client's interests above their own. For example, say a broker represents a buyer. The broker knows something that the buyer does not know that makes the property undesirable. The broker has an obligation to tell the buyer even if it means a lost sale.

**How it is used:** The broker representing the seller explained to the buyer what it meant to not owe their **fiduciary duty** to them.

## inspection report

### a professional physical property inspection

**What it is:** the report prepared by a professional after a physical inspection of the property, focusing on the structure

**How it works:** Anyone purchasing property with a structure on it will likely have some type of inspection done before purchasing it. An investor who purchases a large, complex investment property may also have very specific inspections done for maintenance purposes before or after they take ownership of the property, such as an inspection focused on the building's mechanical equipment. A prospective homeowner will have a general inspection completed either prior to signing the purchase agreement or as a condition in the purchase agreement. Some states have licensed home inspectors, and in other states, buyers may use engineers, contractors, or builders.

**How it is used:** They were able to negotiate a reduction in the price because of some of the problems that were found in the **inspection report**.

## listing

### offering a property for sale

**What it is:** a way to offer property for sale through a real estate agent

**How it works:** The term *listing* is used two ways. In common usage, a real estate agent lists a property or takes a listing. They investigate the property and sign the appropriate agreement to represent a seller. The act of taking a listing creates the listing itself (the submission of the property information to a database shared by real estate agents). Regardless of the usage, listings all refer to the seller's agent placing the property on a list shareable with other agents. The list can be the agent's own personal list of properties, but usually the listing is placed on a multiple listing service, or MLS (a real estate marketing system), serving a particular geographic area. The listing will contain all the property's details. Most agents in the area will belong to that MLS, so all listings are shared among all member agents, increasing opportunities to find a buyer.

**How it is used: Listing** the property for sale turned out to be a good idea because more people could see the details of the **listing**.

## MLS (multiple listing service)

a real estate marketing system

**What it is:** a system for advertising properties for sale among a group of real estate brokers

**How it works:** A multiple listing service (MLS) is a private organization sometimes operated in association with real estate broker associations for the purpose of enhancing real estate marketing opportunities. Brokers (people acting on behalf of the seller) will sign a listing agreement to get the right to sell a property for a client. They will then place the property information on the multiple listing website. Other brokers with buyers can contact the listing/selling broker to arrange property showings. The MLS allows many brokers to access information on all properties, increasing the chances of a fast sale at the best price. Commissions are negotiated with clients, customers, and brokers.

**How it is used:** The broker from the next town was able to locate a great house for the buyer client through the **MLS**.

### negotiation

the process of agreeing on terms

**What it is:** the process by which two opposing parties (buyer/seller or landlord/tenant) discuss the terms of an agreement and hopefully reach a mutually satisfactory conclusion

**How it works:** Purchasing any property will usually involve some level of negotiations. Some simple negotiations include an offer, counteroffer, and acceptance, while complicated negotiations include base rent, common charges, and tenant incentives. Negotiations are often conducted verbally, but until the terms and conditions are agreed to in writing, they hold no legal weight. Despite the importance of price, there may be other issues, such as correcting certain problems in the building, seller financing, and contingencies that must be resolved. If both parties are using real estate agents (people representing their interests in the transaction), it is typical for the offers and counteroffers to be made through the agents.

**How it is used:** The **negotiation** went on for quite a while since the seller was on vacation.

## offer to purchase

### what the buyer is willing to pay

**What it is:** a proposal to buy a property at a certain price communicated to the seller

**How it works:** The offer to purchase is generally in response to the seller's first offer to sell the property for a certain price. However, a buyer may initiate by making an offer on a property not currently on sale. Once the offer is received, the seller may accept it, reject it outright, or reject it with a counteroffer. The buyer is then free to accept the counteroffer, reject it, or reject it with another counteroffer. This process may proceed verbally or in writing. Unless the offers and counteroffers are made in writing, they generally hold no legal weight. Any offer made is automatically invalidated if the other party makes a counteroffer.

**How it is used:** The real estate agent conveyed the buyer's **offer to purchase** to the seller with the seller's agent present.

## open buyer agency

### agent who finds the property gets paid

**What it is:** an arrangement that pays any broker who, as a representative, finds a property for the buyer

**How it works:** In an open buyer agency, a buyer would likely contact several brokers (people acting between a buyer and seller) in the area with the details of the kind of property they want to buy. A broker who found the property would likely want to sign an exclusive buyer agency agreement to represent the buyer for that property to protect the broker's fee.

**How it is used:** The buyer was willing to work with any of the brokers in the area, so they sent all of them the property details with an offer of **open buyer agency**.

## open listing

offering multiple agents the chance to sell the property

**What it is:** one in which the owner agrees to pay a fee to any broker who sells the property

**How it works:** An owner may set up an open listing by contacting several brokers (people acting between a buyer and seller) with the property information and stating an offer to pay a fee to anyone who successfully sells the property. Initially, it is usually an informal arrangement. If a broker locates a buyer, they will then want the seller to enter into some kind of formal agreement so that the broker's fee is protected.

**How it is used:** The owner believed that an **open listing**, allowing multiple brokers to try and sell the property, would best serve their needs.

## probate sale

court-mandated sale when someone dies

**What it is:** the court-ordered selling of property when someone dies without a will

**How it works:** When someone dies without a will (intestate), the court will usually intervene to order the sale of the property for any heirs, or those to whom the estate may owe money. These properties may often be sold at attractive prices since they are usually sold as is, the estate being unlikely to make any repairs.

There are specific requirements about deposits and court approvals of the sale that may make the process cumbersome and lengthy. A probate sale should not be confused with a sale by the heirs of a deceased person, which will be conducted directly either by the heirs or by the executors of the estate.

**How it is used:** The buyer had their eye on a **probate sale** but knew they'd have to wait a while before they could take possession of the property.

## purchase agreement

contract for buying/selling a property

**What it is:** the written contract stating the terms and conditions for sale and purchase of a property

**How it works:** The important thing to know about real estate purchase agreements (also called sales contracts) is that they must be in writing to be enforceable. All states have some version of what is called the statute of frauds, a law that states conditions pertaining to certain types of agreements. So, verbal agreements to buy or sell property cannot be enforced by court action. In most cases, this also applies to leases for more than a year, which also must be in writing. The purchase agreement (sales contract) will contain all the terms and conditions of the sale. A deposit, usually of at least 10% of the purchase price, is usually required at the time the agreement is signed.

**How it is used:** The **purchase agreement** required the buyer to obtain financing within thirty days; otherwise, the agreement would expire.

## Realtor®

creating a membership title

**What it is:** a trademarked term for a member of the National Association of Realtors

**How it works:** The term *Realtor* is a trademarked word that indicates that the user is a member of the National Association of Realtors (NAR). A Realtor and real estate agent are not the same, and they are not interchangeable. It is wrong to call a real estate agent a Realtor unless you know they are members of the NAR. However, the majority of real estate agents are, in fact, NAR members.

**How it is used:** This real estate agent was a **Realtor®**, but Justine had met with a few agents who were not.

## recording

creating a public record

**What it is:** the act of placing a document with a public agency to create a record of something

**How it works:** Real estate transactions are typically recorded in the town, city, or county clerk's office to create a publicly available document of the transaction. The documents usually filed are the deed and the mortgage agreement. Many are under the false impression that if a deed is not recorded, it's invalid. Deeds are valid upon the giving and accepting of the deed. However, should there be a later claim of ownership against the property, recording may make the difference as to whose claim is upheld as valid. Deeds are routinely filed right after closing. The public availability of these documents helps with title searches. Recording fees are usually charged.

**How it is used:** The title company took care of **recording** the deed.

## right of first refusal

### offering property to someone first

**What it is:** a legally binding right to purchase a property before it is sold to anyone else

**How it works:** A right of first refusal results from an agreement requiring the seller to offer the property to the individual named in the agreement before selling it to anyone else. This agreement might be used when a property owner wants to purchase the property next door that is not yet for sale. The agreement may be for a specific price agreed at the time it was discussed, based on an appraised value, or reserved for when the property is offered for sale. Sometimes tenants want to eventually buy the building, or the property owner may want to be paid for granting the right.

**How it is used:** The building owner was able to negotiate a **right of first refusal** for the building next to theirs.

## salesperson

### a person that works for a broker

**What it is:** someone who works for a real estate broker in representing people in real estate transactions

**How it works:** Real estate licensing generally has three levels: broker (the person acting between a buyer and seller or tenant and landlord), salesperson (sales agent), and associate broker (a broker working under another licensed broker). A salesperson is a professional who has a license that allows them to engage in real-estate-related activities only under the supervision of a licensed real estate broker. There are no limits on the types of real estate activities that a salesperson can engage in, as long as all activities happen under and through the broker.

**How it is used:** The **salesperson** advised the seller that the fee had to be paid to the broker and not directly to them.

## seller disclosure

**information revealed by the seller**

**What it is:** a legal requirement that the seller reveal certain information about the property

**How it works:** Seller disclosure is about providing the buyer with physical information about the property prior to the purchase of the property. Seller disclosure rules are state specific. Some states may require very little seller disclosure, while others have general rules about disclosure that might require a lawsuit to prove that the seller knew of a condition like a leaky roof and did not disclose it. Some states have adopted a property condition seller's disclosure form that is either mandatory or requires a fee be paid if the seller refuses to complete the form. Still, other states may have environmental issues like earthquake zones and may require specific disclosure of those conditions.

**How it is used:** The buyer discussed with their real estate agent what they could expect with regard to **seller disclosure**.

## single agency

**one person, one representative**

**What it is:** the situation where a broker represents one person, the client, in a transaction

**How it works:** There are several variations of the agent-client relationship in real estate transactions. The agent is someone who represents someone else in a transaction, and their client is the person being represented. The most obvious and easily understandable is the single agency relationship. A person hires a broker to represent them as a seller, buyer, landlord, or tenant. A salesperson working for the broker may do the day-to-day work involved in representing the client. In the single agency arrangement, the agent, that is the broker and the salesperson (if any), owe their fiduciary duty (loyal representation) to the client. Dual agency is where a broker will represent a buyer and seller (dual agency), and in designated agency, a broker will appoint one agent to represent the buyer and another agent to represent the seller.

**How it is used:** The ABC real estate brokerage represented XYZ Corporation in a **single agency** arrangement.

## tenancy in common

### a way to own property with other people

**What it is:** an ownership arrangement that allows two or more people to own separate interests in the same property

**How it works:** Tenancy in common is one way to own property with one or more other person or people. The property is owned as a whole (no physical divisions), but individuals may own different percentages. The individual percentages may be sold to others and may be left to heirs should the original person die. It is common in condominium ownership for people to own their own unit and own the common areas and buildings as tenants in common.

**How it is used:** The investor decided to include two friends as **tenants in common** in the building ownership by allowing them to invest in the property.

## title search

### a review of the property's history

**What it is:** a review of the current and previous records of the title (ownership) of the property

**How it works:** Because most properties are long-lasting and likely have had multiple owners, past events may have cast doubt (called a "cloud") on the title, or the actual ownership of the property. Most owners take out a title insurance policy to insure them against claims occurring after they've acquired the property.

Before issuing a title insurance policy, the company will conduct a title search to determine if there is any problem with the title that they want resolved before issuing the policy. The search may also indicate an issue that cannot be resolved, and the company therefore will not insure. A lender issuing a mortgage loan will always require the borrower to take out (and buy) a title insurance policy to cover the bank's interest in the property. Title searches may also be done to resolve title claim disputes or to verify ownership before purchasing the property.

**How it is used:** The closing was delayed due to a problem that was discovered during the **title search**.

## transactional broker

one agent working the deal; no representation

**What it is:** when one broker handles both sides of a transaction between two parties without representing either side

**How it works:** In some states, there is a form of brokerage that allows for one broker (the person acting between a buyer and seller or tenant and landlord) to handle a transaction between two parties without representing either party. The idea is to administer the transaction as flawlessly and smoothly as possible, taking no sides between the parties involved. These transactional brokers are often paid a flat fee rather than the typical commission arrangement.

**How it is used:** Since both parties were experienced real estate investors, they agreed to negotiate through a **transactional broker**.

## unilateral contract

only one party is obligated to act

**What it is:** an agreement where one side *may* act and the other side *must* act

**How it works:** A unilateral contract is when a contract is signed giving certain rights to one side and obligations to the other. The most obvious example is a purchase option agreement, where one party is obligated to act but the other is not. For example, party A is interested in buying a piece of property but needs to do more research about the property. So, party A asks the owner, party B, for an option agreement for one year to purchase the property at a specified price. Party B agrees, likely for a fee. During that year, party B may not sell the property to anyone other than party A. During that year, if party A tells party B that they wish to purchase the property, party B must sell to party A. However, party A has no obligation to purchase the property and may simply let the option agreement expire.

**How it is used:** The tenant understood a **unilateral contract** would protect them, so they asked for a lease option to renew the lease at the end of the first five-year term.

## walk through

### the final inspection before closing

**What it is:** the buyer's last inspection of the property before ownership is conveyed at the closing

**How it works:** The walk through allows the buyer one last look at the property before proceeding with the purchase. It is generally scheduled as close to the time and date of closing as possible, often on the same day. The purpose of this final inspection is to make sure the property is in the same or better condition as when the sale was agreed to. It also provides the buyer with a chance to verify that any agreed-to repairs have been satisfactorily completed.

**How it is used:** The buyer and seller agreed to schedule the **walk through** on the morning of the closing date.

# CHAPTER 9

# Financial Analysis

Investment properties are all about money. People who buy investment properties anticipate either an immediate or near-future return on their investment. That return may be in cash or in tax benefits. Either way, the expectation is that the investor will come out ahead financially by buying the investment property.

Financial analysis is a key aspect of evaluating and selecting an investment property. Most financial analysis involves three time frames: past, present, and future. Data from the past three to five years is analyzed for current profit. Current income and costs are processed with projections to estimate future profits for five to ten years. Past data is factual, while analyzing the current data requires consideration of price and investment goals, and future profits are best estimates based on what is known now.

The terms in this chapter will give you an understanding of many of the aspects of financial analysis. Where possible, simple mathematical examples have been provided. As with the whole subject of real estate investment, it's wise to consult an expert to help with financial analysis. However, this chapter should help you understand the process, ask the right questions, and understand the answers.

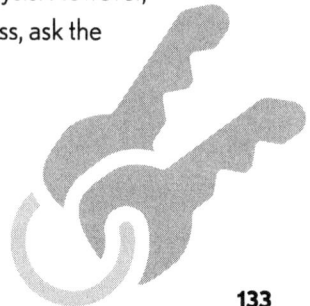

## 80/20 principle

**What it is:** the idea that 80% of the rewards in real estate (or any endeavor) will come from 20% of your efforts

**How it works:** The 80/20 principle (or Pareto principle) is the idea that a small, focused effort (20%) on the right things will generate the majority (80%) of the rewards. In real estate, an investor can examine past successes to understand profit. So, the investor should focus on those opportunities when making new investment decisions. Delegating tasks to free up time to pursue those 20% of opportunities is another application of the principle.

**How it is used:** When looking for the next property to buy, the investor used the **80/20 principle** to preselect only properties that met certain criteria.

## BER (break-even ratio)

income compared to expenses

**What it is:** a quick way to determine what percentage of the investment income will go toward expenses

**How it works:** The formula to calculate the annual break-even ratio (BER) is: mortgage loan payment (debt service) plus all operating expenses divided by effective gross income (money available to pay the bills). So, if a property had mortgage loan payments (debt service) of $20,000, operating expenses of $16,000, and effective gross income of $48,000, the BER would be 75%, or ($20,000 + $16,000) ÷ $48,000. Assuming that all space in the building is rented at the same rate, the building would need to have 75% occupancy to break even. Lenders may consider the BER when making mortgage loans for investment properties.

**How it is used:** The **BER** for the building was 60%.

## capital expenses

large repairs or replacements

**What it is:** the costs associated with large-scale, infrequent property repairs, replacements, and upgrades

**How it works:** Most properties have projects that happen infrequently, like a new roof. These occasional or infrequent projects are generally referred to as capital expenses. Additionally, large improvements to the property, like creating gardens for the use of the tenants, are also capital expenses. These projects help maintain, and sometimes increase, the value of the property. Capital expenses are programmed so that funds can be put aside or be funded by a loan.

**How it is used:** The new owner had already calculated the **capital expenses** of replacing the air conditioning equipment and installing a new furnace.

## cash flow

### money remaining after expenses

**What it is:** the total money remaining after all expenses are paid for a rental property

**How it works:** Cash flow is calculated by subtracting all operating expenses including debt service (payments for the loan) from property income. It can also be calculated by subtracting debt service from net operating income (NOI; property income after expenses). Cash flow can be positive, negative, or neutral. Positive cash flow means there is money left after all expenses. Neutral means that the property breaks even. Negative cash flow means that property income does not cover expenses.

**How it is used:** The investor was concerned with the low **cash flow** of the property.

## cash flow statement

### tracking income and expenses

**What it is:** a report that records regular costs and income

**How it works:** The cash flow statement tracks income and expenses, essentially cash in and cash out. This statement may help in planning for certain expenses based on income and other expenses. For example, suppose an investor owned vacation rentals that had greater use in the summer than in the winter. Tracking cash flow monthly might help them plan on saving up money during the high season and limiting expenses during the lower-occupancy season.

**How it is used:** In looking at the **cash flow statement**, the owner decided to delay the roof replacement until next year.

## COCR (cash-on-cash return)

measuring return on the investment

**What it is:** a percentage that relates the annual cash flow to the cash invested in the property

**How it works:** The cash-on-cash calculation formula is to divide annual cash flow (money remaining after all expenses) by the initial investment in the property, that is, by the down payment and any major repair costs upon purchase. For example, if someone invested $100,000 as a down payment on a property, and the annual cash flow was $12,000, the cash-on-cash return (COCR) would be 12%, because $12,000 ÷ $100,000 = 12%. This tells the investor that by investing $100,000 (regardless of the property's price), they can make a 12% return on the money they've invested. It is one measurement among others that the investor can use to make an investment decision.

**How it is used:** The **COCR** was somewhat low, but the investor expected rents would go up faster than expenses, generating higher cash flow.

## DCR (debt coverage ratio)

the ability to pay debts

**What it is:** a ratio measuring the relationship between income, expenses, and debt service (mortgage loan)

**How it works:** The debt coverage ratio (DCR; also called the debt service coverage ratio) is one of the measurements used by lenders to determine if an investment can generate enough money to pay off its cost. The formula is to divide net operating income (NOI) by debt service. Since NOI is the result of deducting expenses from income, the question becomes: Are there sufficient funds left to pay the debt service? For example, if a property had an NOI of $100,000 and debt service of $60,000, the DCR would be 1.67, as $100,000 ÷ $60,000 = 1.67. The higher the debt coverage ratio the better; lenders will look for a DCR of at least 1.25.

**How it is used:** The bank was satisfied that the **DCR** indicated that they could pay the debt service out of the building's income.

## debt yield

### measurement of income to debt

**What it is:** a measurement that lenders involved in investment real estate use to measure risk

**How it works:** The debt yield measures the relationship between net operating income (NOI; property income after expenses) and the total loan amount. The formula is NOI divided by total loan amount. For example, if the NOI is $50,000, and the total loan amount is $500,000, the debt yield would be 10% because $50,000 ÷ $500,000 = 10%. A higher debt yield is usually better.

**How it is used:** The lender was concerned with the low **debt yield** number for the investment.

## effective gross income

### money available to pay the bills

**What it is:** the term used to identify money available, whether actual or estimated, to pay property expenses

**How it works:** Effective gross income (money available to pay the bills) is an estimated figure included in the pro forma (a projected operating statement). First, property income is estimated at 100% occupancy of the building, regardless of its actual occupancy. This is called the potential gross income. A vacancy and collection loss percentage that is derived from the market is then subtracted from that 100% occupancy number. The result is the effective gross income. Say the potential gross income of the building is $100,000, and the vacancy and collection loss number is 5%. The effective gross income will be $95,000. (First, $100,000 × 0.05 = $5,000. Then, $100,000 − $5,000 = $95,000.)

**How it is used:** The investor ignored the additional parking income when calculating the **effective gross income** to see if there was enough money to pay the bills without it.

## equity buildup

**What it is:** the increase in the equity portion of the property

**How it works:** Equity (the amount of a property's value that you own) is value minus all debts. Two things may happen over time to increase the equity in a property: The property can increase in value through appreciation. The debt can be reduced through payment of principal on the mortgage loan. If an investor had an interest-only loan, there would be no reduction in the principal owed, but the property could still increase in value through market conditions (appreciation). If the property did not appreciate in value but the investor had an amortized mortgage loan, where a portion of the principal is paid off each month, the debt would be reduced, and the equity would grow. Technically, some analysts consider equity buildup the amount of equity that grows through mortgage loan payments. They measure appreciation separately.

**How it is used:** The investor counted on **equity buildup** through paying off the mortgage loan so that the property would be debt free when it was sold.

## equity buildup rate

**What it is:** the percentage that equity grows in the first year of an investment

**How it works:** The equity buildup rate can be calculated for the first year of property ownership by dividing the total increase in equity by the initial cash investment. Suppose an investor put $200,000 down on a property that appreciated in value in the first year by $20,000, and the investor paid off $10,000 of the mortgage loan. Divide that $30,000 total equity buildup (the increase in the equity portion of the property) by the $200,000 initial investment, and the equity buildup rate equals 15%. This calculation is only valid for the first year since equity and equity buildup will likely change from year to year.

**How it is used:** The investor hoped their assumptions would be correct about appreciation since the project would then have an **equity buildup rate** of 20%.

## financial risk analysis

looking at fiscal factors affecting an investment

**What it is:** an analysis of monetary aspects that could negatively affect an investment

**How it works:** Financial risk analysis looks at monetary issues like current interest rates and borrowing terms affecting a potential investment to determine how risky it would be to continue. Most real estate investments are leveraged (using borrowed money); the availability of loan funds at reasonable interest rates can be crucial. Initially, borrowing terms will affect the debt service (payments for the mortgage loan) of the investment. Changing terms can affect borrowing for capital expenses (large repairs or replacements) or refinancing (taking out a new loan on existing property). Another important consideration is whether the property income can cover the debt service. The financial risk analysis considers all these factors in assessing the potential risk of the property from a monetary point of view.

**How it is used:** After doing the **financial risk analysis**, the investor decided not to buy the property.

## IRR (internal rate of return)

a way to compare real estate investments

**What it is:** an investment analysis tool for calculating the annualized rate at which an investment can grow

**How it works:** In simple terms, the internal rate of return (IRR) estimates how much you can profit through your investments. Calculation of the IRR considers the initial investment, time value of money, expenses, income, and future sale price. The result is the percentage rate at which the initial investment can grow. It is a way to compare different investments over different time periods.

**How it is used:** Despite the high **IRR**, the investor proceeded cautiously.

## market risk analysis

**What it is:** an analysis looking at various factors in the real estate marketplace to determine the risk level of an investment

**How it works:** Market risk analysis is one aspect of risk analysis (an overall analysis of the likelihood of the project achieving expected financial goals). It focuses on real estate market conditions in the broad market. It considers where the market is in its usual pattern of growth, stability, decline, and rebound. Market risk analysis focuses on those factors such as high vacancy rates (a measure of available rental space, in this case when there are large numbers of unrented units/homes in an area) which could negatively affect the investment.

**How it is used:** The investor completed a **market risk analysis** before deciding whether to purchase the property.

## one percent rule

**What it is:** a quick way to determine if a property's income can pay the monthly debt service

**How it works:** The one percent rule is a guideline used by rental property owners. The rule states that a property's total monthly income should at least equal or exceed 1% of the purchase price of the property. Initial repair expenses should be added to the purchase price. For example, say an investor was looking at a property that cost $500,000 and needed $10,000 in repairs. One percent of $510,000 is $5,100. As a general guideline, in this example, the income of the building should generate at least $5,100 a month. The one percent rule then backs into the mortgage loan by recommending that the monthly mortgage loan payment not exceed this number. This is a rough guideline and does not consider other expenses and later repairs.

**How it is used:** According to the **one percent rule**, the buyer will need to keep their mortgage loan payment below $7,000 per month.

# OER (operating expense ratio)

**What it is:** a ratio measuring operating expenses against the property income on an annual basis

**How it works:** An investor will look for a property with a low operating expense ratio (OER), because this indicates that the property is being run efficiently and likely profitably. The formula for calculating the annual OER is total operating expense (costs of running the property) minus depreciation and then divided by total income.

Suppose a property cost $600,000 a year to operate, including debt service (mortgage payments). Depreciation for the year is estimated at $100,000 and total income is $800,000, so ($600,000 – $100,000) ÷ $800,000 = 63% OER. Operating expense ratios are subject to market conditions and may vary with different types of buildings; that is, residential versus commercial. In general, the lower the OER, the better.

**How it is used:** One thing the investor made sure to do was to compare the **OERs** of the two properties she was considering.

## operating expenses

**What it is:** the monthly/annual recurring expense items necessary to operate a rental property

**How it works:** Operating expenses as used in the pro forma (a projected operating statement) are projections based on previous years' expenses as well as records for similar properties. The expenses are sometimes broken down into three categories: fixed, variable, and reserves for replacement. Fixed expenses are typically taxes, insurance, and special licenses. Variable expenses are all other recurring expenses except debt service (payments for the loan), which is accounted for at the end of the pro forma. Reserves, or reserves for replacement, are longer-term items the owner is responsible for but not on an annual basis, like a gas range in an apartment.

**How it is used:** The investor had several years' worth of income and expense statements from which to estimate the **operating expenses** for the property.

## operational risk analysis

looking at operational factors

**What it is:** an analysis that examines the factors that may negatively affect the running of the building

**How it works:** An operational risk analysis will focus on factors that may have a negative effect on tenant satisfaction and could therefore create problems with rental rates and high vacancies. Factors such as tenant services, responses to complaints, maintenance and cleanliness issues, and anything else that may impact tenant satisfaction are examined in this analysis. For example, gaps in service, such as maintenance for elevators, cleanliness in shared spaces, and private unit fixes to appliances, heating, or similar items are thoroughly considered. Responses to occupants' complaints are also highly considered.

**How it is used:** The **operational risk analysis** showed a lack of timely response to tenant complaints by the management company.

## P&L (profit and loss) statement

a report on property financial activity

**What it is:** any form or report prepared to summarize financial factors determining the profit or loss in an investment

**How it works:** Profit and loss (P&L) statements are not unique to real estate investment. Any business or investment can, and should, do an ongoing accounting and analysis of expenses and income to determine the profit and loss position at any point in time, as well as over a period of time. A P&L statement for a real estate investment would likely be done monthly to track trends and pinpoint possible problems. The statement would track all income and expenses. The P&L could also be used to project income and expenses in the near future.

**How it is used:** The investor asked the accountant to prepare a monthly **P&L statement** on the new investment.

# PGI (potential gross income)

## income estimate

**What it is:** the estimate used in creating a pro forma (a projected operating statement)

**How it works:** Potential gross income (PGI) is calculated as if the building were 100% occupied, even if it's not. As part of an investment analysis or an appraisal, a pro forma may be completed for a new or completely remodeled building with no tenants, a partially occupied building, or a building with 100% occupancy. Income for the space in the building may be estimated at current lease rents for occupied space and market rents for vacant space. All income is usually included in the PGI estimate, including what is sometimes called "other income," like parking fees and laundry machines. One variation of this is to include additional income after the vacancy and collection loss percentage is applied to PGI. This is because other income may not be subject to the same fluctuations as the regular rental income.

**How it is used:** Most of the below market rent leases were about to expire so the buyer used market rent for the entire building when estimating **PGI**.

## price-to-rent ratio

### indicator of whether it's better to buy than to rent

**What it is:** an analysis comparing median house prices with median annual rents

**How it works:** The price-to-rent ratio is an indicator of whether it's better to rent or buy a home. For the investor, houses may be overpriced in the market if the ratio is too high. The ratio can be calculated for any market area where data is available. To calculate, divide the median home price by median annual rent. For example, if the median home value in an area is $400,000 and the median annual rental is $30,000, the price-to-rent ratio is 13.33. The price-to-rent ratios will vary over time and by region of the country. In general, ratios of less than 15 indicate it's better for the individual to buy and therefore investors may have a harder time finding renters. Ratios above 20 indicate a stronger demand for rentals, which may be good for residential property investors. The ratio can also be used to help determine annual gross rent for an investor by dividing the house price by the ratio common to the area.

**How it is used:** The **price-to-rent ratio** indicated that a monthly rent of $2,500 was fair for the house.

## pro forma

a projected operating statement

**What it is:** a widely used format for making estimated projection of income and expenses for an investment property

**How it works:** The format for a pro forma follows (for a one- to five-year time frame):

Potential gross income (estimated income from the building at 100% occupancy even if vacant) minus the vacancy and collection loss (a percentage estimate used by analysts for nonpayment of rents; usually 5%–10%) equals the effective gross income (the amount of money available for operating expenses). Then, subtract expenses (all operating expenses [like real estate taxes, utilities, and maintenance] except the mortgage loan payment) to get the net operating income (money left over after all operating expenses are paid). Then, subtract the mortgage loan payments (debt service) to get your cash flow (actual cash left before taxes are paid and after all expenses [including mortgage loan payments] are made).

An example would be the potential gross income ($150,000) – vacancy and collection loss of 6% ($150,000 x 0.06 = $9,000) = the effective gross income of $141,000 (you get from $150,000 – $9,000). Then, subtract $40,000 expenses to get the Net Operating Income of $101,000. Subtract the Mortgage Loan Payments of $90,000 to get the Cash flow of $11,000.

**How it is used:** The investor created several **pro forma** projections using different assumptions regarding investments in the building's energy efficiency.

## reserves for replacement

funds for nonrecurring replacement items

**What it is:** the budget item that accounts for things that must be replaced periodically but not annually

**How it works:** In the pro forma (a projected operating statement), the reserves for replacement (also called reserves) account for items that the landlord is responsible for, but that do not need replacement every year. This would place these items in the variable expense line. The calculation for these items involves estimating cost and then prorating (dividing by) the number of years' lifespan of the item. Suppose the landlord is responsible for replacing six apartment refrigerators at $4,000 each and the lifespan is ten years, the amount to be accounted for annually would be $2,400.

**How it is used:** The new owner took extra care to make sure they didn't overlook anything when they put together the **reserves for replacement** budget line.

## return of investment

getting back your money

**What it is:** recouping your original investment plus later expenditures

**How it works:** Return of investment is the concept that an investor should get back at least all money invested in the property. This can include not only the original down payment, but any money invested along the way that did not come out of property income. For example, suppose an investor bought a property for $200,000 down on a $600,000 property. The property was an investment with negative cash flow (money remaining after expenses), meaning it never generated enough money to pay the bills. Each year for six years the investor had to put $5,000 into paying the operating expenses ($30,000 total). For the investor to get the return of their investment, they would have to sell the property for at least $630,000. Anything above that would be a profit, or return on the investment. To keep this simple, there are no closing costs, inflation, and equity buildup included.

**How it is used:** The **return of investment** was the first thing the investor wanted to be sure of.

## ROE (return on equity)

a way to measure profit

**What it is:** the percentage return annually on the amount of equity an owner has in the property

**How it works:** By dividing annual cash flow (money remaining after expenses) by the equity (the amount of a property's value that you own) in the property, you have return on equity (ROE). Suppose an investor made a $100,000 down payment on a property and collected $15,000 in cash flow in the first year. The ROE would be 15%, that is, $15,000 ÷ $100,000. Future calculations would have to consider appreciation of the property and paying off the mortgage loan. Changes in these numbers would change the equity the owner has in the property. Likewise, changes in cash flow due to increased expenses and rents would also have to be considered.

**How it is used:** The **ROE** decreased, so they sold the house.

## ROI (return on investment) cost method

a method of measuring the profit you could make on a real estate investment

**What it is:** a way to understand profit based on total investment costs resulting in lower profitability numbers than the ROI out-of-pocket approach

**How it works:** The cost method of measuring return on investment (ROI), or whether investors make back their money plus any profit, compares the total cost of the property with its current value. Suppose an investor bought a property for $200,000 with a $50,000 cash down payment and a $150,000 mortgage loan and spent another $50,000 improving the property. Now, let's say that with the improvements, the property is now worth $350,000. The profit is $100,000 over the original cost plus renovations ($200,000 plus $50,000). Divide the profit by the total cost, including renovations, of the original investment to get ROI. In this example, $100,000 ÷ $250,000 = 40%. So, after the total cost of the property (owner's cash plus borrowed funds), the owner's profit was 40% in the transaction. No differentiation is made between cash and borrowed money here.

**How it is used:** To determine profit, the owner used the **ROI cost method**.

## ROI (return on investment) out-of-pocket method

a way to measure profit based on actual cash invested

**What it is:** a method for relating equity (actual cash invested) to market value, often resulting in higher profitability numbers than the ROI cost method

**How it works:** The out-of-pocket method of calculating return on investment (ROI; a profitability measure on invested money) divides the initial cash investment plus out-of-pocket renovation costs, by the cash invested. Suppose an investor bought a property for $200,000 with a $50,000 cash down payment and a $150,000 mortgage loan and spent another $50,000 improving the property. That totals a cash outlay of $100,000 for a $250,000 property (price plus renovations). With improvements, the property is now worth $350,000. The profit is $100,000 over the original cost plus renovations. However, for this calculation, only consider how much cash was invested. Divide the profit by the cash (out-of-pocket) invested. $100,000 ÷ $100,000 = 100% profit. The actual dollar profit is the same ($100,000) using either the cost or out-of-pocket method. However, the out-of-pocket method provides a direct picture of how well money is working to produce a profit.

**How it is used:** The investor also used the **ROI out-of-pocket method** to further analyze the property and the profitability of the cash outlay.

## sensitivity analysis

a way to analyze individual elements in an investment

**What it is:** a method by which individual factors are analyzed to determine the feasibility of an investment

**How it works:** A sensitivity analysis first lays out all the important factors in a real estate investment, such as, but not limited to, financing, operating expenses, and income. Then, this analysis makes assumptions about each individual factor. For example, an investor might assume three different levels of debt service (payments for a loan) one at a time to see how they each affect profitability. The investor would do that for all the other factors. Sensitivity analysis is considered a good tool to test various assumptions in judging whether an investment can achieve the investor's goals.

**How it is used:** The investor tested out various rent levels as well as different operating expenses by doing a **sensitivity analysis**.

# CHAPTER 10

# Investment Economics

Investment economics is a very broad topic—one that can be worthy of Nobel-Prize-winning economists. Real estate investment economics is a little narrower, but it can still get into subjects that may seem irrelevant to someone wanting to buy a six-unit apartment building as an investment. To some extent you'd be right.

However, within this chapter, you'll see the relevance in buying that six-unit building to investment economics, because investment economics, especially real estate economics, is about value. And if someone knows about value, hopefully, they can use that knowledge to make profitable investments.

When someone sees the word *economics*, they think of economic studies in university or government discussions of economic theory. The terms in this chapter are not about theory but about human behavior, because it's human behavior that creates value. It's you wanting to rent an apartment in your friend's building because it's such a great space in a terrific location that you're willing to pay top dollar to live there. That's all supply and demand.

This chapter will cover terms like *competition* or *conformity*, as well as others that'll provide a practical understanding of how the economics behind real estate investment works. You can then use that knowledge to invest wisely and profitably.

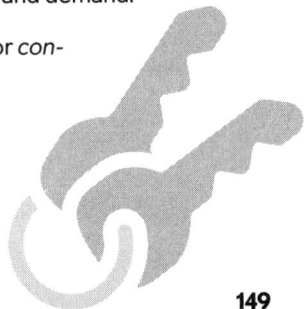

## anticipation

### the value of future benefits

**What it is:** an economic concept describing that all the benefits of owning property occur in the future

**How it works:** A person buys a property today, and so, they set the price of the property today. They will enjoy the benefits of owning that property starting right after closing. If it's the home they live in, those benefits might include a quiet neighborhood or good school systems for potential children. If it's an investment property, that future benefit will be money and possibly tax benefits. Calculations for net present value (the value today of all future benefits of owning the property) and discounted cash flow analysis (a method to analyze the future benefits of owning a property and arriving at the net present value) put numbers and formulas to the concept of anticipation.

**How it is used: Anticipation** of being able to retire using the investment income led the investor to buy a second apartment building.

## balance

### the relationship of the value of the land to the value of the building on the land

**What it is:** in every area, and for every type of property, there is a prevailing balance between the value of the land and the value of the building

**How it works:** In any area, the ratio of land to building achieves a balance over time. In one neighborhood, land values are in the $100,000 range and most properties with homes on them are selling for $500,000. That means the land value to building value ratio is 20%, as 20% of the total value is the land value. If someone were to buy a piece of vacant land in the area and build a small, $100,000 house on it, they would be underdeveloping and wasting a profit opportunity. On the other hand, if they built a million-dollar house, they would likely be overbuilding and may have a hard time selling the house, unless the neighborhood was changing.

**How it is used:** The land value to building value ratio was so out of **balance** in the area that it was being redeveloped with more expensive homes.

## change

**What it is:** the economic concept that things don't remain constant over time

**How it works:** Buildings wear out. Architectural styles go in and out of fashion. Retail sales move from stores to the Internet. Jobs change to allow for remote work, requiring less office space. People age and need different living arrangements. These are just some of the changes seen over the course of a lifetime. While an investor cannot predict or change the future, they can observe the changes happening and try to anticipate how profits can be made through wise investment choices.

**How it is used:** The change in the area seemed to indicate the need for more luxury rental apartments.

## capital flow

**What it is:** in real estate, this term refers to movement of money among and between investors and lenders and buyers and sellers of goods and services

**How it works:** Capital flow is not limited to real estate investors, but for the purposes of this book, the term describes the buying and selling of goods and services between real estate investors and other businesses. A property owner hiring a cleaning company is an example of capital flow. An investor rehabilitating an entire building by resourcing goods from a variety of building suppliers is also capital flow.

**How it is used:** The real estate economy was very good, resulting in good capital flow to the building industry.

## competition

**What it is:** in real estate, this term describes suppliers (developers) competing for the same demand dollar

**How it works:** Suppose that a demand develops for something, say retirement homes in a warm climate area. The supply side (real estate developers, agents, and others involved in land development) see the demand and try to supply what's needed, namely retirement-style homes. The supply side competes for that demand dollar until the demand is satisfied. Because the supply side moves slower than the demand side, a surplus sometimes develops when demand is satisfied.

**How it is used:** The **competition** to build office space was fierce and no one anticipated the remote work trend.

## conformity

### value is affected by things being the same

**What it is:** in real estate, the concept that value is created and supported by things being similar

**How it works:** When someone buys their single-family home to live in, they want to be surrounded by other single-family homes, preferably ones that are similar in design and size. When someone owns an office building investment property, they want it to be in an area that has other office buildings and commercial uses. They don't want to be in the middle of a residential neighborhood.

Buyers will create value to be in these conforming neighborhoods, and they will want to pay less if the property does not conform to ones around it. Note that conformity does not mean being exactly the same. It means similarity in things like land use, building use, and design.

**How it is used:** The investor looked for a commercial building that had a high degree of **conformity** with the neighborhood.

## contribution

### something is worth what it's worth

**What it is:** the value of something may not be the same as its cost

**How it works:** Value is set in the marketplace according to supply, demand, availability of capital, and a variety of political and socioeconomic conditions like war, employment rates, and government policies. In real estate, though value is related to cost, the amounts are not necessarily the same, especially in remodeling. Suppose a homeowner spends $50,000 finishing their basement. Though it may raise the value of the house, you can't assume that the value will be raised by the cost to finish that basement. The principle applies to an investment property. An improvement to a property might allow the owner to increase the rents, which could increase the building's value. The amount in which the value increases is a function of the marketplace and not the cost of the improvement (another example of the principle of contribution).

**How it is used:** The investor was aware of the principle of **contribution** when he decided to remodel the bathrooms in all six apartments to be able to raise the rents, raising the building's overall value.

## demographics

### studies of population characteristics

**What it is:** studies of various characteristics of a group of people

**How it works:** Demographic research involves two things: what you want to know about people and what group you want to study. From a real estate perspective, demographic studies may be driven by population trends that then create investment opportunities. For example, by studying the age of a population of an area, a developer may conclude that they should build one-story homes. Building this type of home would allow people to grow older without having the issues related to climbing stairs. Or study income levels to determine if building a luxury store makes sense.

**How it is used:** The developer wanted to know the income, age, and marital status **demographics** of the region to plan the apartment sizes in their new building project.

## effective demand

### the ability to buy what you want

**What it is:** the financial ability to have the marketplace respond to what you want

**How it works:** People want things. Whether or not they have the buying power to obtain those things is what effective demand is all about. Someone may want a million-dollar home. That's demand. But unless they have a million dollars, the market will not respond to their demand. No one will sell them a million-dollar home for less than a million dollars, and no builder will build them a million-dollar house for less. In real estate, effective demand is enhanced by leverage, or the use of borrowed money. Mortgage loan money is usually readily available. For real estate, effective demand is a combination of buyer funds and borrowed money. So, lower interest rates will increase someone's effective demand because they can borrow more while not increasing loan payments.

**How it is used:** Once interest rates went down, everyone's level of **effective demand** went up.

## externalities
### the monetary worth of location

**What it is:** the real estate term for the influence that location has on value

**How it works:** Beyond the property and building itself, there are many factors outside of the property affecting its value. For example, access to public transportation and highways, convenient parking, support services like restaurants and convenience stores, public safety, and local property tax levels are all external factors that can affect the value of an office building. The value of a single-family house may be impacted by externalities such as the school system, parks, and distance from essential shops like grocery stores and pharmacies.

**How it is used:** The **externalities** that affected the property did not make this a particularly good investment.

## highest and best use
### a way to describe highest value

**What it is:** the use that will bring the highest value for the property

**How it works:** Highest and best use is the idea that each piece of land has a single use that is legally allowed, physically possible, and the most productive economically. "Legally allowed" refers to private and public land use controls. "Physically possible" means that the property is large enough and is otherwise physically appropriate for the use. "Most productive" means that it is the use that will generate the highest income if there is more than one use that meets the first two criteria.

**How it is used:** The investor determined that the **highest and best use** for the property would be to build single-family homes.

## increasing and decreasing returns

### a dollar spent is not necessarily a dollar back

**What it is:** the concept that for every dollar that is spent on construction or improvement, there will be a monetary return above the cost up to a point

**How it works:** The idea behind increasing and decreasing returns is that at the beginning of a project, a dollar spent will generate more than a dollar of value. However, a point will eventually be reached when overbuilding begins to occur. At that point, for every dollar spent, less than a dollar in value will be achieved. The point where the shift occurs is very dependent on the area, quality of construction, and intended market audience.

**How it is used:** The developer was able to maximize **increasing returns** and avoid **decreasing returns** by researching the area and carefully planning out project costs.

## inflation

### the loss of buying power

**What it is:** a decrease in the value of money in terms of what it can buy

**How it works:** An example of inflation is something that cost one price ten years ago now costs a higher price simply because of time passing. In real estate investment, rents are collected over a period of years and appreciation (increase in value of the property) is only realized when you sell the property at a future date; so, time ultimately affects the actual profitability of the investment.

Let's say you can buy a car today for $40,000, but you then choose to put that money into buying a house. In ten years, you sell the home you bought and make a $40,000 profit. However, now the very same car model as before costs over $48,000 because of a 2% per year inflation rate. A real estate investor can't control inflation, but when projecting income, expenses, and profit, they need to be aware of the loss of buying power over time and should take steps to compensate.

**How it is used:** As long as the **inflation** rate stayed low, the owner believed they could make reasonable rent increases to stay profitable.

## liquidity

### converting an investment to cash quickly

**What it is:** a description of how fast a person can cash out an investment

**How it works:** Though not unique to real estate investing, liquidity is integral to the investing field. Liquidity refers to how fast a person can get their money out of any investment. For example, a personal checking account is highly liquid. Money in stocks, though less liquid than a checking account, are still considered relatively liquid in that they can be sold quickly. Real estate is not considered a liquid investment. The term *illiquid* is sometimes used. Under normal circumstances, it takes time to market and transfer ownership of a property, at which point the seller gets cash.

**How it is used:** The investor knew that real estate had very low **liquidity**, so they were careful to keep a cash reserve rather than invest all their money.

## opportunity cost

### the cost of choices not made

**What it is:** the loss of income or profit from investments that are not made

**How it works:** Opportunity cost illustrates that there are multiple opportunities for investment. This is important because people try to make investment decisions to offset the lost chances they had. For example, say you can get a 5% return on a US Treasury bond. This is a no-risk investment. So why would you invest in real estate if your anticipated return was only 5%? The answer is that you wouldn't. You'd expect to get 5% *plus more* to pay for the extra work and risk of a real estate investment.

**How it is used:** The bond market was paying a 5% safe return, so the investor had to calculate that lost **opportunity cost** when considering making a real estate investment.

## real estate bubble

### an unusual rise in real estate prices

**What it is:** an unsustainable rise in real estate prices due to demand exceeding supply

**How it works:** A real estate bubble (or housing bubble) can affect any type of real estate. The bubble can occur for various reasons, but the root cause is usually high demand with limited supply, forcing prices to rise. When mortgage interest rates are low, the possibility of home ownership increases, and a housing bubble can occur. The market generally corrects itself at some point, but the consequences for individuals can be a significant loss of value in the property and sometimes loss of property through foreclosure.

**How it is used:** The investor had bought at the height of the **real estate bubble** and was struggling to pay the mortgage loan.

## progression

### benefiting from more expensive properties

**What it is:** the economic theory that a property benefits from being in an area of more expensive properties

**How it works:** Progression describes the advice to be a small house in a big house neighborhood. The value of a property is affected by the value of the properties around it. A small home or investment property may benefit by being surrounded by larger, more expensive homes or buildings. For example, say a small house in a neighborhood of larger homes is worth $400,000, but in a neighborhood of similar, smaller homes might be worth $300,000. The reason for that difference in value may be due to land costs, the viewed prestige of the neighborhood, amenities like parks and higher-rated schools, etc. There's no hard and fast percentage benefit to progression. Each situation is unique. This phenomenon is the opposite of regression.

**How it is used:** The investor was counting on the benefits of **progression** when they bought the house to rehabilitate and rent in the more expensive neighborhood.

## regression

### don't be the biggest or best

**What it is:** the economic theory that the value of a property will suffer by being in a neighborhood of less expensive properties

**How it works:** Regression is when a property will suffer a loss in value because it is larger and more expensive than the properties in the neighborhood. There is no formula for the actual loss in value, but say you have a house that could be worth $500,000 in a neighborhood of $500,000 homes. In a neighborhood of $300,000 homes, that property might only be worth $400,000. Regression indicates that the lower-value properties will pull down the value of the larger, more expensive property. Regression is the opposite of progression.

**How it is used:** The investor was not aware of the concept of **regression** when they rehabilitated the house to double the size of the other homes in the neighborhood.

## substitution

### similar properties will have similar values

**What it is:** the concept that properties with similar features, what's sometimes called utility (usefulness), will have about the same value

**How it works:** Substitution is key in appraisal work and pricing properties through comparative market analysis (CMA). The theory of substitution is that by studying the actual sale prices of similar properties, you can estimate the cost of an additional unsold similar property. If three six-unit apartment buildings recently sold for $2,000,000 each, another six-unit building with the same features, in the same neighborhood, will likely sell for a similar price. The analysis process can be complicated with different property details, but appraisers and real estate professionals are trained in estimating value using the principle of substitution.

**How it is used:** The appraiser applied the principle of **substitution** when using the sales comparison approach to estimate the value of the residential property.

## supply and demand

### what you have and who wants it

**What it is:** the concept that balances how much there is of something against how many people want it

**How it works:** Supply in real estate is limited. In any neighborhood, there's limited land, houses, apartment buildings, and office buildings. Depending on many factors, a few, some, or a great many people may want to live or work in that neighborhood. The relationship is: High supply and low demand equal low prices. Low supply and high demand equal high prices. Demand is driven by many factors, which are different for different types of properties. Areas with good schools will be in high demand for residences. Areas with good transportation and parking will be desirable employment areas.

**How it is used: Demand** was high in the area for vacation homes, and the prices were going up quickly because the **supply** of new homes was low.

## underwater

### relationship of value to mortgage loan amount

**What it is:** an expression used when the amount of the mortgage loan on a property is greater than the value of the property

**How it works:** People don't usually put themselves in an underwater financial position, nor do lenders knowingly allow it. In normal financing, a buyer is permitted to borrow a portion of the value/sale price of the property. In some cases, a lender will lend 100% of the value, usually for single-family homes with some kind of mortgage insurance. A property being underwater occurs when the property's value goes down due to economic conditions to the point where the remaining balance on the mortgage loan is greater than the possible selling price of the property.

**How it is used:** In the last recession, many homeowners found themselves **underwater**.

# CHAPTER 11

# Governmental Issues

The activities of real estate development, redevelopment, purchase, sale, investment, and management are all subject to one form or another of governmental involvement. Most of the time, the involvement is local, meaning at the town, village, or county level. There is sometimes another layer of regulation at the state level.

The federal government doesn't involve itself very much in actual regulations, but it may provide funding through grants that may help a real estate development project. The federal government is also very involved in taxation issues that may affect real estate investment. Mortgage loan guarantees are another way that the federal government can help a developer trying to sell new homes. Some of these items have been covered in other chapters.

Because most governmental involvement in real estate is at the local level, specific rules and regulations will vary by state as well as municipality within a state. The terms in this chapter will provide you with a general understanding of the way governmental issues can affect real estate investment. These definitions will guide you to understanding your local laws and regulations. They will also help in asking the right questions of local officials, especially if you are new to real estate investment.

## affordable housing mandate

a requirement to build affordable housing

**What it is:** a requirement that a developer include a certain number of affordable units in their development

**How it works:** An affordable housing mandate is a requirement put into place by a community, stating that a housing developer *must* designate a certain percentage of the units as affordable when being rented or sold. So, if a 10-unit building was mandated that 10% be affordable housing, 1 unit must be classified as such. Some communities allow the developer to contribute to an affordable housing fund instead of designating the required number of units. A mandate is required, making it stronger than a policy, such as a policy encouraging inclusion of affordable housing units with bonus numbers of units or subsidies.

**How it is used:** The town's **affordable housing mandate** required that 10% of the units be offered at affordable prices.

## affordable housing policies

encouraging construction of affordable housing

**What it is:** ways the government can help provide reasonably priced housing in their community

**How it works:** In many communities, the average price of housing is too expensive for the average person to buy or rent. All government levels can enact policies that encourage/require affordable housing units to be built. To encourage developers to build affordable housing, government programs can include many different incentives. Affordable housing policies include grants, low-interest loans, rent subsidies, mandates (required housing units), bonuses (additional units above the normal number allowed), and direct construction by the government with government funds. For example, a federal grant may be given to the town to put in the sewer and water lines needed to serve a new development. This grant relieves the developer from these costs. Preferential access to these units is often given to local government employees.

**How it is used:** The town's **affordable housing policy** allowed the builder to add 10 more units to their project if 7 were designated as affordable units.

## architectural board

### public agency managing building design

**What it is:** a board dealing with design issues in a community

**How it works:** A community's architectural board (or architectural commission or architectural review board) may be asked to review and approve all new and remodeling construction from a design perspective. Not all communities have architectural review boards, and a board's duties and powers may vary from one community to another. In some communities, they only advise on the construction of public buildings like a library. In others, they might only review commercial construction, or they may review and deny permits for any construction.

**How it is used:** The **architectural board** required the developer to change their design to fit in with the rest of the neighborhood.

## building code

### regulations governing construction

**What it is:** a regulation providing minimum standards for new and remodeling construction

**How it works:** Building codes are often adopted at the state level. Local municipalities are required to adopt the same or a stricter code. These codes are minimum codes for safe construction. They may also contain regulations dealing with environmental issues like insulation and windows. Homeowners sometimes complain that they shouldn't have to follow building codes since they live in the home. The object of the code is not only to protect the current homeowner or visitors, such as customers in a commercial building, but also all future owners, adjacent property owners, and safety personnel (e.g., firefighters).

**How it is used:** The town **building code** required insulation of the basement if the homeowner wanted to finish it for living space.

## building permit

**What it is:** the local government's approval of building plans indicating that the proposed construction meets all requirements

**How it works:** An architect or engineer will prepare plans for someone who wants to build or remodel a structure, then submit the plans to the local municipality with a building permit application. The municipal officials will review the plan, and if it meets all the requirements of the applicable codes, the officials will issue a building permit allowing construction to proceed. Municipalities have different requirements for their building permits, and these permits will cost more or less depending on the location and project.

**How it is used:** It was several weeks from when the application was made that the **building permit** was issued.

## drainage regulations

**What it is:** local municipal ordinances that deal with controlling water draining from one property onto another or onto public areas like streets or sidewalks

**How it works:** With drainage regulations, the general rule is that any water (runoff) coming from a property must stay on the property and be dealt with. The goal is to prevent flooding or damage to another property or municipal sewer facilities. Large, open surburban areas are of particular concern, but urban areas may also be affected. Various methods may be required in new or remodeling construction to deal with these issues. A developer should be aware of drainage regulations as any needed changes will cost time and money.

**How it is used:** The town just implemented **drainage regulations** for any new construction over 500 square feet.

## environmental regulations

**What it is:** regulations specifically dealing with development and land use issues that may affect the environment

**How it works:** Environmental rules and regulations exist at many levels from federal to local. The regulations that affect development generally are found at the state or local level. Some rules, like building insulation requirements, will be found in the building code. Other regulations may be found in a separate environmental regulation ordinance. Still others, such as wetlands regulations, may have their own ordinance. These ordinances are designed to promote conservation of resources, like energy, and to protect the environment from the possible negative effects of development.

**How it is used:** The **environmental regulations** required that all trees that were removed during construction had to be replaced wherever possible.

## Fair Housing Act

federal law prohibiting housing discrimination

**What it is:** the 1968 federal Fair Housing Act, as amended, makes discrimination in the sale or rental of housing illegal

**How it works:** The Fair Housing Act, which can be found at the federal Department of Housing and Urban Development (HUD) website, contains two primary components. The first is the things you can't do, like refusing to rent to someone, and the second is the list of protected classes, which are the characteristics on which you can't discriminate, like race or religion. There is also a short list of exceptions where protected classes (other than race) are involved. In the case of race, the 1866 Civil Rights Act has no exceptions and remains the law. In some cases, states and local municipalities have supplemented the federal law with stricter laws.

**How it is used:** Since the owner was going to self-manage their apartment building, they wanted to make sure they knew all the requirements of the federal **Fair Housing Act**.

## FAR (floor area ratio)

how much can be built on a property

**What it is:** a measurement based on the property size as to how much floor area will be permitted

**How it works:** Communities develop floor area ratios (FARs) to control overall building size. To calculate the FAR, divide the gross floor area of the building by the total property size. For FAR purposes, the gross floor area of a building will include all floors above ground and in some cases below or partially below ground. So, if a building has 40,000 square feet of space on a 10,000-square-foot lot, 40,000 ÷ 10,000 = FAR of 4. To apply the FAR, multiply the lot size by the FAR. So, if a lot is 30,000 square feet and the FAR is 3, a building of 90,000 square feet would be permitted (30,000 × 3). The FAR is primarily used for commercial properties, but some communities apply it to residential properties as well.

**How it is used:** The **FAR** was 0.15, meaning they could build a 6,000-square-foot house on the 40,000-square-foot lot.

## government subsidy

government money available for a project

**What it is:** the government sometimes provides funds directly to a builder or a community to help accomplish a public good

**How it works:** A direct government subsidy of money may help to build or rehabilitate a structure, providing a benefit to the public. For example, a state government may provide specific funds to pay for the infrastructure for a new affordable housing project. A state or local government might provide a direct funding subsidy or low-interest loan to people buying and rehabilitating homes in a run-down neighborhood. However, there may be a requirement for the buyer/rehabilitator to live in the home for a certain period of time to avoid speculation.

**How it is used:** The developer applied for both state and local **government subsidies** to build their affordable housing project.

## green building

a building with minimal environmental impact

**What it is:** this building type is characterized by certain features that reduce its impact on the environment to a minimum

**How it works:** Green buildings are built to conserve natural resources like energy and water. These buildings use renewable resources like solar and wind power wherever possible. In their involvement at each stage of its life cycle (construction, operation, reconstruction, and deconstruction), the builders and owners of green buildings strive to have a minimal impact on the environment and its resources. There are several certifications for green or energy-efficient buildings. Different green buildings may impact the environment around them in different ways too. For example, one green building may have plants growing outside to encourage biodiversity, while another creates an excess of solar energy.

**How it is used:** The fact that this was a **green building** made it popular with prospective tenants concerned about the environment.

## license law

regulations regarding certain professions

**What it is:** individuals performing real estate–related activities for another person are regulated by each state

**How it works:** State governments (not local or federal) regulate certain professions and occupations that serve the public. By requiring education and experience before granting a license, the government assures a minimum level of competence when hiring someone. Real estate brokers, salespeople, and appraisers all have varying levels of licensing requirements imposed by states. Property managers, inspectors, escrow agents, title closers, and title searchers may all have separate licensing requirements in different states.

**How it is used:** The investor's friend, who was not a licensed broker, offered to help them buy an investment property for a small fee, but the investor knew this would be a violation of **license law.**

## municipality

a geographic, legally defined governmental area

**What it is:** a local area defined by law that is governed by some form of elected body

**How it works:** The term *municipality* is generally used to refer to towns, cities, villages, boroughs, and sometimes counties. A municipality has a governmental structure and can pass its own laws. Technically, while states and counties are municipalities by this definition, this term often refers to local governments. From a real estate investment perspective, most development controls like zoning and building codes are adopted and implemented at the municipal level. Jurisdictions, that is, the power over a geographical area, may overlap. For example, a developer might have to comply with the local town laws as well as county and state regulations.

**How it is used:** The developer checked the zoning in several towns to determine which **municipality** would allow them to build the 10-story office building.

## municipal agencies

organizations within the government

**What it is:** various organizations, boards, and departments within the local government that implement government regulations and policies

**How it works:** Local governments, like the state and federal government, have elected officials who pass the laws and make policy. These are passed down to various units within the government to implement. Municipal government within a state tends to have similar agencies responsible for the same actions. But these duties, and even the names of the agencies, will differ from state to state. It is important for a real estate investor, especially one who is also a developer or remodeler, to know which agency does what and what approvals are needed in the property's municipality.

**How it is used:** The new developer visited the town hall to get an idea of what **municipal agencies** they would have to deal with to get their project approved.

## permitting

getting government permission to do something

**What it is:** the process governments use to control certain activities

**How it works:** Many activities require government approval; this is the government's way of preventing activities that may not be safe or compatible with other activities, like building a factory in a residential neighborhood.

It's also the way governments safeguard the public by imposing standards on various activities. The use of the term *permit* usually involves a single activity, such as a building permit (government approval to begin construction) to construct a building. Sometimes it can involve an ongoing activity, such as a health department permit to operate a restaurant. Permits involving real estate investments tend to be controlled at the local and state level. Other laws exist at the state and federal level that affect real estate investments but do not require permitting, like fair housing laws.

**How it is used:** The **permitting** process to reconstruct the wetland was very slow.

## redlining

### denying loans by location

**What it is:** the illegal practice of denying housing loans by location

**How it works:** Redlining, engaged in by some lenders, is the practice of automatically denying a person a mortgage, home equity, or construction loan because of the property's location rather than the individual's credit and the value of the property. When this was more common, redlining resulted in pushing property values down because buyers couldn't get a mortgage loan. Then, properties were neglected because the owners couldn't get loans to rehabilitate or upgrade them. Minority neighborhoods were especially targeted by redlining. The term comes from the practice of drawing a red line around certain neighborhoods. It's now illegal at the federal level.

**How it is used:** Evidence of **redlining** by a lender could bring federal charges of discrimination.

## steering

### illegally guiding people to certain neighborhoods

**What it is:** the illegal practice by some real estate agents of guiding people to some residential neighborhoods and away from others as a means of discrimination

**How it works:** Steering is often done very subtly by advising some buyers that "they would be happy in this neighborhood," or telling other buyers that "this is not the neighborhood for them." Sometimes it is done more obviously. Any feedback about a particular house or neighborhood *must* be based on cost and the buyer's finances. Any other factor, like race or religion, is viewed as steering and is illegal under federal law. While a buyer technically may ask discriminatory questions and not be subject to any penalties, a real estate agent may not answer those questions because of steering, and the agent would be subject to penalties.

**How it is used:** The buyers got the feeling that the agent was **steering** them to a particular neighborhood because they were African American.

## subdivision

### dividing one property into more than one

**What it is:** the process and the result of dividing one property into multiple properties for development and sale

**How it works:** A single property must be legally divided for pieces of it to be sold. Subdivision is the process of applying for and obtaining government approval to subdivide the property; it only applies to the land division process. The result is referred to as a subdivision. This generally takes place at the municipal or county level. Rules are in place for items like road patterns, drainage issues, street lighting, and other elements common to subdividing properties and creating separate lots. Overall, subdivision authority is controlled by the state. Therefore, the approval process will usually be the same within a state, but it may vary between states. A particular local agency will be designated as the subdivision approval authority. After subdivision approval, development is subject to all other applicable codes and regulations.

**How it is used:** The developer applied for a 10-lot **subdivision** for the 15-acre property.

## variance

### an exception to the zoning regulations

**What it is:** a unique, one-lot exception to the zoning ordinance as it applies to a particular piece of property

**How it works:** Zoning regulations are applied equally to all properties in a community in a particular zone. Occasionally, a piece of property has unique features that make meeting the zoning requirements difficult or impossible. For example, zoning might require a building to be constructed at least 50 feet from the road, but a stream running through the property makes that impossible. In these cases, the owner can apply for a variance that would allow construction closer to the road. The agency deciding on the variance has different names, such as the zoning board, zoning commission, and zoning board of appeals. Physical and personal hardship may be reasons to grant a variance.

**How it is used:** The builder wanted to locate the building closer to the back property line because of the rock outcropping in the front of the property, so they applied for a rear yard setback **variance.**

## wetlands

### special drainage properties valued for their environmental benefits

**What it is:** properties that have special characteristics that help prevent flooding

**How it works:** Wetlands are state- or local-government-designated areas that are preserved because of their environmental benefits. A wetland's soil, location, and vegetation can absorb more water than the average property. They become important in preventing flooding of other properties. The wetland and its buffer areas are generally prohibited from being developed. Wetlands may be in public ownership, but designation of wetlands on private property is common. Construction on properties containing wetlands is often subject to review by special municipal agencies such as a wetlands commission.

**How it is used:** The developer was prevented from using the entire property because of the presence of **wetlands.**

## zoning board

### public agency that deals with zoning issues

**What it is:** usually a group of volunteers in a county, town, city, or village who are appointed to deal with various zoning matters

**How it works:** The zoning board is generally an advisory board to the chief-elected officials in a community. They also may be responsible for granting variances. The zoning board may also be known as the zoning commission or zoning board of appeals. Since its duties are dictated by state law, the functions of the zoning board typically will be the same within any state. However, its duties may vary from one state to another.

**How it is used:** The owner applied to the **zoning board** for a variance from the maximum building height requirement.

## zoning laws

laws controlling land use

**What it is:** local government controls over how land is used

**How it works:** A municipality's zoning laws (or ordinances or regulations) control land development. A community is divided into zones by the type of land use that is permitted, such as residential, office, retail, industrial, etc. The zones may be further divided by density, or how much of a particular use may be built on a given piece of property. For example, one residential zone may permit apartment buildings, while another may only permit single-family homes. Zoning generally works the same in various communities. The differences will be in the specific types of zones and regulations within those zones.

**How it is used:** The **zoning laws** permitted 10 units per acre, so the developer thought the property might be good for low-rise garden apartments.

# CHAPTER 12

# Structure and Mechanicals

This chapter will define terms that relate to the physical structure and mechanical systems of various kinds of property. As with many of the other terms in this book, the definitions will provide an introductory understanding of words you may come across as you explore real estate investments.

The physical elements defined in this chapter can be very complicated when in their actual physical setting. The definitions here will help you understand what questions to ask and what some of the answers mean as you investigate properties that might be suitable investments.

Experts play an important role in the design, construction, and maintenance of the structures and mechanicals that are defined here. It's especially important to hire the right professionals to thoroughly inspect any investment property that you might be interested in. This chapter should help you understand what the professionals have to say.

One note before you read further: In most cases, the definitions deal with the basic idea of what is being defined. In real estate, size matters. This means that an air conditioning system can be anything from a small unit in the basement of a house to a gigantic system to cool a 100,000-square-foot office building. The goal is to provide a basic understanding of what these systems do and why they may be important.

## building materials

the physical supplies (not tools) used to construct a building

**What it is:** those items that go into the construction of the structure itself

**How it works:** Building materials are those items that become part of the structure as it is being built. For example, concrete can create the foundation for a building, while lumber creates the structure of a home. Building materials are commonly distinguished from things like mechanical equipment. Innovations in building materials are constantly being made. Most material's usage requires experience or special expertise. Welders working with steel on high-rise building construction need special training and may need a license in certain states and cities. Innovations in materials sometimes allow for different design options. Often, older buildings need to be renovated (and it's more cost efficient to do that renovating) with newer materials.

**How it is used:** We were waiting for the **building materials** to be delivered to get started on the roof framing.

## construction cost

amount of money needed to build something

**What it is:** the total amount of money it will cost to build something not including land purchase

**How it works:** Construction cost generally describes the cost to build a structure without land acquisition costs. Development cost, however, usually means the entire cost, including land, to complete a project. Construction costs are often stated in dollars per square foot, but this may be inaccurate because costs vary based on location, quality of materials, and special features in the structure. Cost per square foot is initially useful for comparison or estimating purposes. A detailed construction cost estimate is based on material and installation (or hard) costs. Design, supervision, and other "soft costs" (like permitting fees), are included in a final cost estimate. While land acquisition costs aren't part of the construction estimate, land development costs might be.

**How it is used: Construction costs** were much cheaper where the developer's previous project was located.

## electrical panel

the starting point for electric power distribution

**What it is:** the point where electric power comes into the building and is distributed into different circuits

**How it works:** The electrical panel (or electrical distribution panel/distribution board) is where various individual circuits begin and are controlled for power distribution throughout the building. Each circuit on the panel is connected through a circuit breaker that cuts the power to that circuit in the event of a problem with that circuit. In much older buildings, the protection device was called a fuse, and the panel was called a fuse box. You can't add up the amperage rating of each circuit breaker to determine the total power to the building.

**How it is used:** The **electrical panel** was installed as soon as the building was sealed from the weather.

## electrical system

system to distribute electrical power

**What it is:** a way to bring electricity into the building and, through a system of wires, distribute it throughout the building

**How it works:** The electrical system is measured by voltage (volts) and amperage (amps). The system distributes electricity to light fixtures, wall sockets, and switches for basic office or residential use. Where additional electrical power may be needed, dedicated lines (single purpose) may be installed which could serve the building's air conditioning system or a large computer facility. Electrical wiring is initially installed after wall framing is complete. Electrical power is usually provided by private or public entities.

**How it is used:** The builder double-checked that the size of the **electrical system** could handle the medical equipment that would be installed.

## energy management system

system to conserve energy

**What it is:** any system designed to help a building manager or owner conserve energy resources

**How it works:** Energy management systems can be data collection software that enable managers to track energy use. They can also be automated systems for controlling various energy uses including HVAC (heating, ventilation, and air conditioning) functions. However, the function of data collection systems is to enable managers to take advantage of energy-saving opportunities. For example, monitoring a furnace's poor efficiency may result in replacing it with a better model, increasing operational cost savings.

**How it is used:** The property manager hoped that the new **energy management system** would lead to a substantial reduction in energy use.

## foundation

### the structure that everything is built on

**What it is:** the lowest part of the building structure, upon which everything else is built

**How it works:** The foundation of a building is part of the structure resting directly on the ground. For large buildings, the soil must be suitable to handle the weight of the structure. The foundation is proportional to the size of the building. A typical house foundation must go down to the depth where the soil freezes. A very large building may have a foundation several stories belowground. Reinforced concrete is the most common material used for foundations.

**How it is used:** The excavation for the **foundation** was complete.

## framing

### the skeleton of the structure

**What it is:** the structural element that outlines the exterior and interior walls of the structure

**How it works:** Framing starts from the outside in—it's like a skeleton on which the exterior and interior walls will be attached. In multistory buildings, wall framing must be completed so floors can rest on the frame. In most homes, the framing is wood, but in larger buildings (like residential and commercial), steel, aluminum, and wood are used for framing. After the foundation is built, framing is usually the next step.

**How it is used:** The weather was good, so the **framing** was completed quickly.

# fuel

an energy resource

**What it is:** an energy resource that, in the context of real estate, is the power to drive something, like machinery, to perform a function

**How it works:** Buildings can be large consumers of energy or fuel. Lights are powered by electricity, which is not strictly considered a fuel but is a possible replacement for most other fuels. HVAC systems can be powered by fuel oil, natural gas, propane gas, and electricity. Even if a system is powered by one fuel, it may require another. For example, an oil- or gas-fired hot water heating system may still require electric pumps to pump the hot water where it's needed, as well as an electric igniter to light the oil or gas. Different fuels have varying levels of efficiency or cost.

**How it is used:** The cost of all **fuels** had gone up so much that the owner was considering supplementing electricity with solar panels.

# HVAC (heating, ventilation, and air conditioning)

climate control in a building

**What it is:** a common term used to refer to various systems in a building that provide climate control and ventilation

**How it works:** The term *HVAC* is a general reference to all systems in a building that deal with air handling and climate control. The same air handling distribution system (ducts) is often used for ventilation and providing warm and cool air where needed. HVAC systems for single-family homes, apartment buildings, and commercial buildings may differ and involve hot water radiation systems or air handling equipment. Energy efficiency is a major issue in the development of HVAC systems.

**How it is used:** The investor hired an **HVAC** specialist to inspect all the heating, ventilation, and air conditioning systems in the building that was under consideration for investment.

## infrastructure

### the physical support system outside the property

**What it is:** the general term used to describe public facilities that support development of a community

**How it works:** Private investment in real estate requires physical facilities that support all types of real estate development. Things like roads, water, sewer lines, public parks, and water and sewage treatment plants, among other public facilities, are part of the community's infrastructure. These facilities are usually paid for through a combination of taxes and usage fees. Sometimes private development may pay for expanding the infrastructure, such as when a developer must extend a sewer line to serve a development.

**How it is used:** The town's **infrastructure** was going to be a major part of the new master plan study that was being proposed.

## land development cost

### cost to create buildable land

**What it is:** costs that account for potentially necessary work to create a property that can be built on

**How it works:** Some pieces of property are practically ready to be built on, depending on the property's state or the intended use. Other properties may require extensive work to create what is called a buildable site or lot. The work might include tree removal, excavation, grading (leveling) of soil, dynamite blasting, rock removal, and construction of retaining walls to hold soil in place. You may also need to bring additional soil to the property. Land development costs are usually treated separately but can also be included as an item in construction costs.

**How it is used:** **Land development costs** for the project were unexpectedly high because of all the rock on the property.

## load-bearing wall

### a wall that has something resting on it

**What it is:** an exterior or interior wall that supports something above it

**How it works:** Buildings are constructed with some exterior walls only used to enclose the building, while other walls are structurally necessary to hold up something above them like the roof. Some interior walls divide spaces into rooms, while others do this and are also necessary provide structural support. Load-bearing walls are often not obvious. Sometimes the ceiling covering must be removed to determine if a wall is load bearing. A wall should never be removed until it is determined whether it is load bearing. If it is, it should only be removed by competent tradespeople with a design in place to compensate for its removal, keeping the building structurally sound.

**How it is used:** They called in a structural engineer to determine if the ceiling was a **load-bearing wall** before removing it.

## mechanical equipment
### items necessary for building operation

**What it is:** items installed in the building that aren't part of the structure but are needed for building operations

**How it works:** Mechanical equipment is best understood as different from the structure itself. Mechanical equipment is generally installed near the end of construction or after a building is complete. While the equipment may be installed in an apparently permanent manner, it is usually removable or replaceable. It generally does not have a lifespan as long as the structure itself. Mechanical equipment can include air conditioning and heating equipment, the elevator, and any solar or wind turbine electrical generating equipment.

**How it is used:** The older building's **mechanical equipment** was all original installations, so the property manager was concerned about setting funds aside for replacement.

## plumbing fixtures
### the things you use that involve water

**What it is:** the items used in the course of business or residence that involve the use and disposal of water

**How it works:** Plumbing fixtures are those items like sinks, toilets, and bathtubs that serve the needs of the people using or living in the building.

Factories, or other types of businesses, may have specialty plumbing fixture needs like large washing stations. Plumbing fixtures are generally installed (connected) on the outside of the walls after the walls are closed in after the piping has been roughed in behind the walls. The term roughed or roughing in describes the process of connecting the main water and sewer pipes from their initial entry point into the building to the individual places like kitchens and bathrooms where the fixtures will be installed. In commercial installations, distribution piping may be more exposed.

**How it is used:** The **plumbing fixtures** were delivered and ready to install.

## plumbing system

piping system for handling water and sewage

**What it is:** a system providing a way to distribute clean water throughout a building and carry wastewater out of the building

**How it works:** Plumbing systems provide two basic functions in a building. The first is to provide and distribute clean, potable (drinkable) water throughout a building. This includes water for drinking, bathing, cooking, and other uses requiring clean, potable water. The second function of a plumbing system is to carry wastewater out of the building. Sources of wastewater include sinks, toilets, showers, and baths. A variety of materials including copper and plastic piping are used. Plumbing installations are subject to government codes.

**How it is used:** Now that all the interior framing is finished, the **plumbing system** can be installed.

## roughing

preliminary work for various systems

**What it is:** a term describing the wall preparation done before work in electrical, plumbing, and other systems

**How it works:** In roughing (the verb being "to rough in"), the distribution systems for electric and plumbing are installed in the walls after the framing is complete but before the walls are closed with the final wall finish. The wires and pipes are usually installed before the insulation is installed. Systems such as phone, cable TV, and sound systems are also roughed in while the walls are open. Roughing brings the connection beyond where the wall will be installed, so that plumbing fixtures and electrical outlets and switches can be connected after the walls are closed in.

**How it is used:** The **roughing** for the plumbing was finished ahead of schedule, so just the electric had to be **roughed in.**

## sanitary sewage
### the dirty water that comes out of a building

**What it is:** the product and process of dealing with the contaminated water that comes out of a building

**How it works:** Sanitary sewage is when the wastewater that comes out of a building, that is, sewage, is not sanitary, but must be treated in a sanitary manner to prevent contamination and illness. The source of the sewage is toilets, sinks, showers, and in industrial buildings, waste relating to certain mechanical or chemical processes. The sewage from most commercial and residential buildings goes into public sewer systems and ends up in sewage treatment plants. Where industrial processes are involved, the wastewater may be pretreated or stored for removal by truck. When public sewers are not available, septic systems are used.

**How it is used: Sanitary sewage** disposal would not be an issue for the new homeowners once the sewer line was extended.

## septic system
### on-site sewage disposal

**What it is:** a system to deal with sewage (wastewater) from a building on the property itself

**How it works:** In areas where there are no public or private sewer lines leading to sewage treatment plants, individual on-site sewage disposal systems are created. These systems consist of septic tanks that receive all the wastewater from the building. Solids settle in the tank and the liquid flows into the septic field. The septic field, also called the leach field, consists of pipes or channels underground where the wastewater seeps into the ground. A septic system is used primarily in residential areas that have no sewers.

**How it is used:** The developer could not reasonably connect to the town sewer, so each home had to have a **septic system** installed.

## sheathing

### outside wall covering

**What it is:** any material that can be attached to the framing on the outside of the structure

**How it works:** The primary objective of sheathing is to provide rigid covering on the outside of the building to which the final finish, like shingles or siding, can be attached. This step happens after the framing of the building is finished. Plywood, oriented strand board (OSB), steel or aluminum panels, and concrete-based panel products are commonly used for sheathing. Rigid panels that provide insulation and water and moisture resistance may also be used.

**How it is used:** After the framing, they installed the **sheathing**.

## smart building technology

### use of advanced computer systems to manage certain operations

**What it is:** technology that uses software and hardware to monitor and control building operations

**How it works:** Through the use of sensors, artificial intelligence, and other developing technologies, an owner can collect data and control systems within a building. The smart building technology goals are tenant comfort, safety, and efficiency of operations. Proper use of smart building technologies should result in greater tenant satisfaction while lowering building operation costs, especially in fuel and energy use.

**How it is used:** The owner was adamant about hiring a property manager who was experienced in **smart building technologies**.

## storm sewage

### disposal of rainwater

**What it is:** water that comes from rain and must be disposed of to avoid flooding

**How it works:** Most storm sewage is dealt with on roads with large storm sewers to remove rainwater quickly, avoiding flooding. Storm sewage, while not clean water, is considered to be less contaminated than sanitary sewage and is therefore usually not treated at a sewage treatment plant but drained directly into lakes, rivers, or the ocean. Some storm sewage originates on private property from rain falling on the property and structures. The term *runoff* is used to describe water hitting the ground and not penetrating, or water falling on structures. Currently, most environmentalists and building officials believe that runoff should be contained on the property. Various structures can be used to contain runoff, such as retention ponds (artificial ponds to contain water) and spreader structures (stone-filled trenches to catch building runoff).

**How it is used:** Communities have tried to minimize the amount of **storm sewage** coming from private property by adopting drainage rules and regulations.

## sustainability

### ability to provide energy needs internally

**What it is:** the capability of a building to provide for its own energy needs

**How it works:** When the energy needs of the building are provided for without purchasing energy or fuel from an outside source, it's demonstrating sustainability. Whether at 100% or a lesser fraction, sustainability is usually a combination of energy-efficient construction and technologies allowing for the production of electricity. Effective insulation and windows and energy-efficient heating and cooling units are part of sustainability. Use of solar panels and wind turbines to generate electricity are the other part. Though it has a different meaning, the term *green building* is sometimes used interchangeably with the term *sustainable building*.

**How it is used:** The owners emphasized the **sustainability** of the building when they advertised space for rent.

## water supply

### providing nontoxic water for the property

**What it is:** the source of safe (potable) water for all property uses

**How it works:** Potable water (or drinking water) generally comes from one of two sources depending on the location of the property and local infrastructure (the physical support system outside the property). One source is some type of community water service. This means that water from a public or private water source, a reservoir, is carried through pipes in the street to a piped connection to the building. This water is often metered so that the owner may be charged according to usage. The second method is through a well on the property. This involves drilling down until water is found and then piping it and connecting to a pump into the building. A well is the owner's responsibility. Responsibility for public water piping may begin at the property boundary or at the connection to the water main in the street.

**How it is used:** The buyer still needed to find out whether they would have to drill a well or if there was a public **water supply** to the property.

# CHAPTER 13

# Flipping

The definition of house or property flipping is far simpler than the process itself, which is why there is a chapter of terms associated with flipping. Flipping is a type of real estate investment where someone buys a building, rehabilitates it in some way, and sells it for a profit.

The intention of flipping is important. The property is not being bought for the owner to live in or use for their business. The intention is clear from before the property purchase is made: The property is meant to renovate and sell for a profit, most of the time. You'll see some variations of the flipping model in this chapter that you may not see on the TV flipping shows.

The criteria for selecting the property is very important, since not every property in need of renovation is a good candidate for flipping. Terms associated with property selection and the flipping process are defined in this chapter. Flipping is best known as an investment in residential properties. Commercial properties of all types can also be flipped.

It's suggested that the reader supplement reading this chapter with other chapters that contain information about government control, financing, buying and selling, mechanical and structural issues, and valuation. Several items in each of these chapters will relate to the process of flipping.

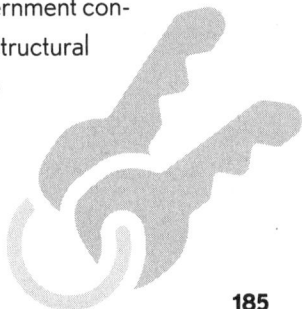

## ARV (after repair value)

### value of the property after renovation

**What it is:** the market value (not total cost) of the property after renovations are complete

**How it works:** After repair value (ARV) is the principle of contribution, where renovation cost doesn't necessarily equal the value added to the property. Say you bought a property for $200,000 that was worth $250,000, and then you did $50,000 in renovation. Upon the project's completion, the after-renovation value was $350,000. There are calculations that can be made to determine profit. But the number that concerns this definition is $350,000, as that is the value (regardless of cost) of the property after the renovations were completed. Remember: These numbers could go a completely different way, with the same property valued at the $250,000 purchase price and $50,000 in renovations only adding $40,000 in value. This would result in an ARV of $290,000.

**How it is used:** The **ARV** guaranteed a profit on the flip if they could sell the property quickly and not let the real estate taxes accumulate.

## as is

### property as it stands

**What it is:** a real estate advertising term that means the seller assumes no responsibility for the condition of the property

**How it works:** "As is" indicates that the owner will make no repairs or guarantees with respect to the property's current state. The buyer assumes all responsibility for the property with no recourse to the seller. The term is often used when marketing a property that requires extensive repair or renovation. It may or may not be livable. An inspection would likely be carried out, but there may be unseen poor conditions. The property will likely be sold below market value for the area and may be a good candidate for flipping depending on the extent of renovations required.

**How it is used:** The investor thought the property that was advertised **as is** might make a good flip—until they got the inspector's report.

## buy-and-hold flipping

### not selling renovated property immediately

**What it is:** when a flipper renovates a property and doesn't sell it immediately in the traditional flipping strategy

**How it works:** A buy-and-hold flipping strategy involves two possible tactics. One is timing the market to maximize profit. A flipper can buy a below market price property, do the renovation work, and then hold the property anticipating a rise in property values that will generate greater profits when the property is sold. A second tactic is to buy, renovate, and then rent the property for the medium- or long-term. Both techniques could be combined with the flipper holding and renting the property for a few years, then selling at a high point in property values.

**How it is used:** The investor decided on a **buy-and-hold flipping** strategy, renting the property until market conditions improved.

## cosmetic renovation

### surface-level changes

**What it is:** changes that are more decorative, faster, and cheaper

**How it works:** Cosmetic renovations tend to focus on those items that are quicker, cheaper, and more visible to potential buyers. They often bring greater profit relative to their cost. Examples of cosmetic renovations would be painting the walls and outside of the property, adding molding, upgrading the kitchen with new hardware, installing new faucets and mirrors in the bathroom, putting in new or refinished flooring, and improving landscaping, among other things. These changes come with higher payouts, as making a place look nice generally makes it more desirable.

**How it is used:** The investor looked for a house to flip that only needed **cosmetic renovation.**

## contractor

### the person who does the work

**What it is:** tradespeople who do the renovation

**How it works:** In construction, contractor can be used in two ways. A contractor hired to oversee a number of different tradespeople is usually called a general contractor or, simply, the contractor. The people that the general contractor hires are usually referred to as subcontractors or "subs." The flipper has the option of hiring a general contractor who will be responsible for the entire project, or assuming the role of general contractor and hiring various tradespeople themselves.

**How it is used:** The investor wanted to get bids from at least three **contractors** for the project.

## fixer-upper

a real estate marketing term referring to a property needing work

**What it is:** a term used in real estate advertisements and listings to indicate a property that needs some level of renovation

**How it works:** A fixer-upper is livable as is, but any property with this description needs repair and renovation—oftentimes at least a little of both. These properties are usually sold below the market value of the area in which they are located, and they may therefore be good candidates for flipping. The decision to flip will depend on the types and cost of the necessary repairs and the house prices in the local market.

**How it is used:** The **fixer-upper** turned out to be more of a teardown since it needed extensive foundation repairs.

## fix and flip

the classic flipping strategy where the house is immediately put up for sale

**What it is:** the most well-known flipping strategy of buying a property: renovating it and selling it at a profit

**How it works:** Fix and flip has several conditions for it to work. The property is usually purchased at a discount price from other properties in the neighborhood. Ideally this is because of issues with the owner, for example, financial problems, rather than significant problems with the property itself. The renovations to the property should add value and not be expensive repairs. For example, repairing foundation problems does not add the same kind of value that upgrading a kitchen would. Finally, the total purchase price of the property, plus renovations and profit, should result in a resale price in line with neighborhood property values.

**How it is used:** The investor spent a lot of time trying to find the right property for their **fix and flip** project.

## flipping costs

### price to accomplish a property flip

**What it is:** total costs including everything from purchase to sale of a flipped property

**How it works:** The costs to flip a property will vary depending on the intended flipping strategy. Looking at a straightforward fix and flip's costs will include all costs to purchase the property, like real estate agent fees, closing costs, inspection fees, and any financing fees. Renovation costs should include any architectural costs and permit fees. Since the property will be owned for a period of time between purchase and sale, there will likely be property taxes due, insurance costs, and ongoing utility fees during renovation or when showing the property for sale. Real estate agent fees and closing costs are also part of the total flipping costs.

**How it is used:** The investor was careful to keep track of all expenses so they could have an accurate idea of total **flipping costs** when calculating their profit.

## flip profit margin

### amount of profit made in a property flip

**What it is:** the amount of money left over after the sale of a renovated flipped property

**How it works:** The basic profit calculation is the after repair value (ARV; the sale price of the renovated property) minus its purchase price, and minus renovation costs. If you could sell a renovated property for $400,000 that you bought for $250,000 and spent $50,000 renovating, your profit margin would be $100,000. Calculating a percentage, you would divide the profit by the selling price, so $100,000 ÷ $400,000 = 25% profit margin.

**How it is used:** The investor wanted at least a 30% **flip profit margin** to make the project worthwhile.

## live-in flip

renovate while you occupy

**What it is:** a flipping strategy where a person lives in a home while they renovate it for sale

**How it works:** The idea of a live-in flip is to have a place to live while doing a flip project. The project is somewhat easier if the house contains more than one dwelling unit, as one can be occupied while the other is being renovated. One advantage of the live-in flip is taxes. Once a property is occupied for more than a year, any profit is taxed at the lower long-term capital gains rate or not at all if the occupancy time is sufficient to claim the residence capital gains tax exclusion. The other advantage is being able to time the sale to take advantage of good market conditions. A disadvantage is having to live with renovation work constantly happening.

**How it is used:** The family needed to move anyway, so they decided to try a **live-in flip**.

## market analysis (flip)

looking at the market for flipping property

**What it is:** an analysis that considers various factors in decisions related to the project

**How it works:** Flipping provides the opportunity to respond to market forces and trends to maximize profit, so any flipper should consider the market forces and desires. Renovation trends, area pricing, identifying the target buyer, buyer or seller's market conditions, cost versus profit potential, and demand for the property are among the factors that a market analysis will focus on. The analysis will help in deciding whether to undertake a flipping project and, if so, what renovations make sense.

**How it is used:** The **market analysis** for a possible flip indicated that the investor needed to cut back on the renovation cost.

## market timing

### best time to sell

**What it is:** being aware of various factors that create good and better marketing conditions for selling flipped property

**How it works:** Once a flip project begins, the sooner the investor sells the property the better, as it will minimize holding costs like insurance and taxes. Seasonal trends are arguably the most fluid and changeable over the short run. Spring and summer in many places are the best times to attract buyers for residential property. Longer market trends like interest rate fluctuations and supply and demand issues can especially affect nonresidential property flipping. The renovation should stick to its timeline.

**How it is used:** The investor planned to complete the renovations of the flipping project to coincide with **market timing** for a quick sale.

## property inspection (flip)

### detailed examination of the property

**What it is:** a review of a possible flip property focusing on the profitable renovation work to be done

**How it works:** All property considered for purchase should be inspected by a professional. The inspection will be the same for someone buying the property to live or work in as it will be for an investor. The difference comes in how that information will be used. As a general guideline, the flipper will be looking for a structurally sound building that may have been neglected or not kept up to date. The flipper will look at the inspection report and make their own inspection with an eye toward renovations that can be done at a reasonable cost, enhancing the desirability and therefore the value of the building.

**How it is used:** The investor inspected the property themselves before ordering a professional **property inspection**.

## pyramiding

### using one building to buy another

**What it is:** using the equity in one property to purchase another

**How it works:** Strictly speaking, pyramiding is not classic flipping, but it's part of the flipping strategy that may be used to create a real estate investment portfolio. In a pyramiding/flipping strategy, an investor buys a property at a below market price and renovates it. But instead of selling, the investor rents it until there is enough equity (the amount of a property's value that you own) to refinance the property and buy another below market property to renovate and rent. Properties can always be sold, but the idea of pyramiding is to develop multiple rental income streams.

**How it is used:** The market had changed favorably, so renting the recently renovated building made sense as the first step in a **pyramiding** strategy to own multiple buildings.

## REO (real estate owned)
### lender-owned properties

**What it is:** a term used to refer to properties that the lender (usually a bank) continues to own after a foreclosure sale has failed

**How it works:** A lender will foreclose on a property for nonpayment of the mortgage loan. It will then usually try to sell it at a foreclosure sale. If they are unable to sell it at the foreclosure sale, they will consider it real estate owned, or REO. The lender will continue to try and sell the property using various methods to market the property, including the use of real estate agents. The properties are often sold at a deep discount, often "as is," and they may require extensive work to make them livable.

**How it is used:** The investor looking at properties to flip contacted several lenders to see if there were any **REO** properties for sale.

## renovation
### modernizing a building

**What it is:** a process that focuses on modernizing a building with technological, architectural, and design changes

**How it works:** Renovation is where a building is brought up to current standards of use and visual appeal. Technological changes, such as a new heating system, might be included in the renovation. The term *gut renovation*

is used to describe the most extensive type of renovation within the shell of the building. Preservation of the architectural or historic character of the building, if any, is not a significant issue. Rehabilitation, on the other hand, does concern itself with preserving the character of the building while upgrading for modern use. In common usage, the terms *renovation* and *rehabilitation* are sometimes used interchangeably.

**How it is used:** Since the building had no architectural significance, the investor decided on a complete **renovation.**

## renovation appraisal
### before and after value estimate

**What it is:** a term used to determine the value of the renovated property before and after the flip

**How it works:** An appraisal estimate of the value of a potential flip property may be made to determine if, and how much, the renovations will add to the value of the property. An appraisal is made at the time of purchase. A "what if" appraisal is then made of the property based on the proposed renovations; in other words, what will the property be worth if the renovations are completed. This is sometimes called a before and after appraisal.

**How it is used:** The investor decided to hire an appraiser to do a **renovation appraisal** to see how much the proposed renovations would add to the value of the property.

## renovation permit
### code compliance permit

**What it is:** a license may be required according to local codes for renovation work

**How it works:** Communities generally require code compliance for all types of construction, including some aspects of renovation and rehabilitation. For example, it's unlikely that a permit is required for interior painting. However, it is very likely that a permit will be required to install a new kitchen. Renovation work is treated no differently than new construction for code compliance. It just tends to be more focused on individual projects.

Renovation can also trigger upgrades in other aspects of the property, for example, installing smoke alarms throughout the house. Future buyers may require proof of proper permitting.

**How it is used:** The investor met with the building department official to determine what **renovation permits** would be needed for the work.

## resale value

### how much is it worth after renovation

**What it is:** the price that the property will sell for immediately after renovation

**How it works:** The resale price of the flipped property is one of several elements that are crucial to flipping. It's important that the resale value is not significantly higher than the general values of properties in the neighborhood. One way to look at this is to work backward from the neighborhood values. In other words, after buying the property and renovating it, you want to end up with a value that is in line with neighborhood prices, while still building in a profit.

**How it is used:** If the renovations were not too extensive, the **resale value** of the property would allow for a reasonable profit.

## return on flipping investment

### money made from the flip

**What it is:** the percentage of profit based on how much money was invested in the project

**How it works:** The calculation for return on a flipping investment is as follows: Selling price of the renovated property minus total costs equals net profit. Then, net profit divided by total cost gives the return on investment.

So, if an investor buys a property for $250,000 and spends $50,000 in renovations costs, their total investment is $300,000. If they then sell the property for $400,000, their net profit is $100,000. Profit of $100,000 ÷ $300,000 investment = 33% return on investment. Most flippers look for a 10% to 20% profit on a project.

**How it is used:** The investor wanted a **return on flipping investment** of at least 15%.

## selling process

### differences in selling flipped property

**What it is:** selling a renovated (flipped) property presents different issues than selling one that is not a flip

**How it works:** Because the property has been renovated and upgraded, several issues in the property may present themselves. Buyers will likely want to see all permits and approvals of the work done. Likewise, inspections may be very detailed out of concern for quick-fix, cheaply done work. Marketing will want to emphasize the modern features of the renovations. Pricing can also be a challenge since renovations and profit margins may have pushed the price to the higher end of prices in the neighborhood.

**How it is used:** The investor interviewed several real estate agents to be sure to hire one that was familiar with the **selling process** for a flip.

## seventy percent rule

### a guideline for calculating profit

**What it is:** a suggested calculation used by property flippers to calculate profit margin and the cost of the investment

**How it works:** To use the seventy percent rule, the investor first must estimate the projected sale price of the property after repair. This is commonly called the ARV, the after repair value. The seventy percent rule states that the investor should pay no more than 70% of the ARV for the property, considering renovation costs. A formula for this would be: ARV multiplied by 0.7, then subtract estimated renovation costs to get the maximum purchase price.

For example, an investor estimates that the property they are looking at will sell for $400,000 after renovation. Seventy percent of $400,000 is $280,000. Assuming the cost for repairs is $30,000, that number is subtracted from $280,000. According to that calculation, the investor should pay no more than $250,000 for the property ($280,000 − $30,000 = $250,000).

**How it is used:** The investor looked at more than 20 properties before they found one where the **seventy percent rule** worked.

## staging

**What it is:** taking physical steps to make a property appear appealing to prospective buyers

**How it works:** Staging can be done for any property for sale, but it is primarily done for homes. Staging for a flipped property can begin with the renovation itself, choosing neutral colors for paint and installing fixtures and hardware that will accommodate most people's decorating sense. Staging usually involves creating a sense of what rooms might be used for, so bringing in furniture is usually a good idea. Whether decorated or left undecorated, space should be clean and free of clutter or debris from renovation. Staging exists as an occupation within the real estate industry.

**How it is used:** The investor decided to avoid **staging** the property to emphasize its spaciousness and to save some money.

## target market

who wants the property

**What it is:** that group or groups of people who will want the renovated property

**How it works:** To some extent, when flipping property, the target market drives the flip. If market demand comes from first-time homebuyers and interest rates are very high, a flipping project targeting that group may not be feasible until interest rates go down. If the office space demand is from relatively small companies not looking for large spaces, the renovations will create those spaces and target that market when advertising the project. The target market is the market that has created a demand that the flipper can satisfy.

**How it is used:** The **target market** in the area was retirees, so the investor decided to install elevators in the two-story units they were renovating to flip.

## turnaround time

time from beginning to end of a renovation project

**What it is:** the time it takes to purchase, renovate, and sell a flipped property

**How it works:** A flipper may count the beginning of the project from the search for the right property, or from the actual day of purchase, since that's when costs begin to accumulate. The end of the turnaround time is when the property is sold. For the fix and flip strategy, the shorter the turnaround time, the better. There are certain costs like insurance, interest on financing, utilities, and property taxes that accumulate over time having nothing directly to do with the renovation work. The faster the renovation is complete, and the less time on the market for sale, the lower these accumulated costs.

**How it is used:** The investor had everything in place, including the renovation team, to be able to shorten the **turnaround time** to six months if the real estate sales market cooperated.

## wholesale flipping

quickly selling properties for flipping

**What it is:** selling property contracts to other people to do traditional flipping

**How it works:** Unlike traditional flipping, the initial buyer does no actual renovation work. Their role is to locate discounted properties suitable for flipping, get a sales contract on that property, and then sell the contract to a third party who will do the necessary renovations and do a traditional flip sale. Wholesale flippers make their profits on the difference between what they paid for the property and what they sell it for.

**How it is used:** The contractor kept contact with several investors who did **wholesale flipping**, hoping to find properties that could be renovated for a quick sale.

# Index

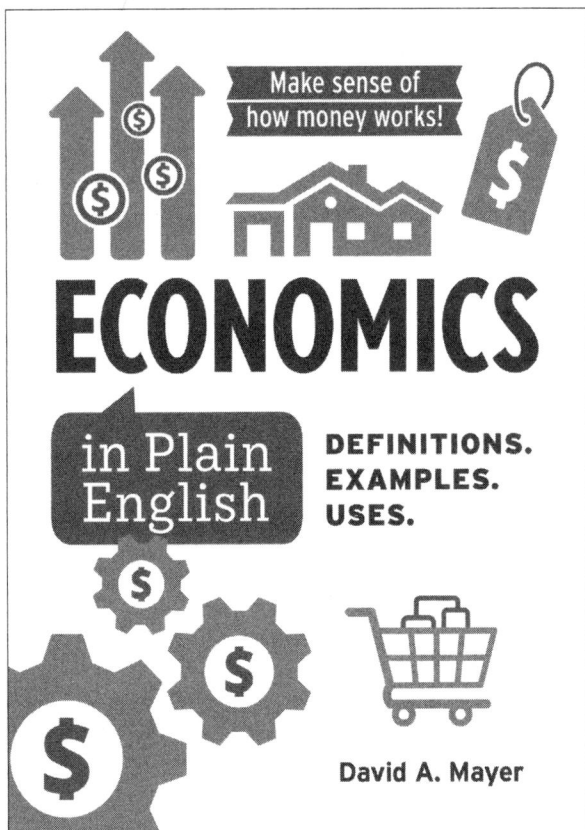